THE NATIONAL ASSOCIATION OF
FLOWER ARRANGEMENT SOCIETIES

COMPLETE STEP-BY-STEP

FLOWER
ARRANGING
COURSE

THE NATIONAL ASSOCIATION OF
FLOWER ARRANGEMENT SOCIETIES

COMPLETE STEP-BY-STEP
FLOWER
ARRANGING
COURSE

DAPHNE VAGG

EBURY PRESS
LONDON

First published 1993

Reprinted 1995

3 5 7 9 10 8 6 4

First published in the United Kingdom in 1993 by
Ebury Press
Random House, 20 Vauxhall Bridge Road, London SW1V 2SA

Random House Australia (Pty) Limited
20 Alfred Street, Milsons Point, Sydney
New South Wales 2061, Australia

Random House New Zealand Limited
18 Poland Road, Glenfield
Auckland 10, New Zealand

Random House South Africa (Pty) Limited
PO Box 337, Bergvlei, South Africa

Random House UK Limited Reg. No. 954009

A CIP catalogue record for this book is available from
the British Library

ISBN 0 7126 3756 7

Special Photography by Marie-Louise Avery

Editor: Alison Wormleighton
Designer: Kit Johnson
Illustrator: King and King
Typeset by Textype Typesetters, Cambridge
Printed and bound in Singapore by Tien Wah Press

CONTENTS

INTRODUCTION

Most of us, at some time or another, have picked flowers, or bought them, and put them in a pot. As children it may have been buttercups or bluebells in a jam jar; later we may have used mother's glass vase for daffodils or grandmother's jug for roses in summertime. The reasons for doing this will have varied: to enjoy the colour or scent at close quarters: to have time to appreciate the beauty and texture of the flowers; to enliven a bare corner in a room or to welcome guests to a dinner table.

Whatever the reason, this is the beginning of all flower arranging. It is often a barely understood desire to do something more with them and to create a new beauty, and this pushes us on to further arrangements.

In the past 50 years flower arranging has developed into a popular art (or craft, if you prefer) for men and women of all ages and interests. Of course there have always been people who have delighted in bringing in their treasures from the garden or have gone home from a country walk with a bunch of pussy willow to enjoy indoors, but it was not until the latter part of the 20th century that so many men and women began to enjoy this as a hobby to be pursued at all sorts of levels.

Flower clubs began to mushroom soon after World War II ended, inspired by the work of Constance Spry, Julia Clements and Mary Pope, who became the Founder President of NAFAS, The National Association of Flower Arrangement Societies, which was formed in 1959.

More than 30 years later NAFAS has a membership of 104,000 in 1350 affiliated clubs. Early club names included the description 'flower arrangement society' or 'floral art group' indicating their origins in local horticultural and gardening societies. Many still do, but by the 1980s newer clubs were simply calling themselves 'such and such flower club'. It was a significant change, reflecting the fact that gardens were smaller, or even non-existent for the increasing number of flat-dwellers who still maintained their love of flowers and foliage, whether fresh or preserved – or even artificial.

The membership of the National Association remains predominately female but the number of men is steadily increasing. Of the 100 demonstrators who have achieved national status within the organization, 30 are men.

The interest (one could truthfully say *passionate* interest) in arranging flowers is by no means confined to the United Kingdom. In many countries there are flower clubs that are now members of WAFA, the World Association of Flower Arrangers, founded in 1981. The stewardship and administration of this organization started with NAFAS in Great Britain, then after three years passed successively to Belgium, France, Canada and New Zealand. In each three-year period the host country holds a residential course for at least one week and an international show.

So it is obvious that flower arrangement goes much further than just putting a bunch of flowers into a vase of water. That is where this course starts. It introduces the reader and arranger to the whole range of the craft, from very simple beginnings, through different styles and techniques, to large displays. You can acquire the props and know-how as you go along.

The course will give you a very sound and comprehensive basis on which to build your flower arranging in the future. If you are not already a member of a flower club, find out about your local one and go along to see a flower-arrangement demonstration. If you cannot get the address and the day it meets from your local library, either telephone NAFAS at 071-828 5145 or write to The National Association of Flower Arrangement Societies, 21 Denbigh Street, London SW1V 2HF.

Chapter One

MAKING A START

*The course starts, as all good lessons should, with something that is
already familiar and can be achieved straight away. But it suggests that you
look a little more critically at what you are doing with flowers –
and why – and how you can improve even the simplest arrangements.
It also encourages you to take an interest in the colour, shape and lines of
what you are using, to develop the 'seeing eye' that artists in any medium must
have, and to begin to understand the wide-ranging interests that flower
arrangement can lead to in design, display, history and allied crafts like
collage, interior decorating and gardening.*

*B*efore you go on to extend your flower arranging, you need to understand the basics, including what tools and equipment are needed at the start and which can be acquired later; what containers to start with; how to make stems stay where you want them to (known as the mechanics); and how to choose, buy, cut and condition flowers and leaves to get the best life from them.

Essential Tools and Equipment

There are a few tools of the trade that you will need right at the beginning. (The figures in brackets in the following text refer to items shown in the photograph on page 10.)

CUTTERS

Kitchen scissors and/or garden secateurs will do to start with. Later you will want to replace them with cutters you keep specially for flower arranging. *Flower scissors* have short blades, one of which is usually serrated, with a nick in the blades that will cut wire. *Loop-handled scissors* (**26**) are generally used for ikebana (Japanese-style arranging) but they make sturdy cutters for any arranger. *Orange-handled secateurs* (**19**) are popular with some arrangers. They have short, pointed blades which enable you to cut precisely when trimming florets, dead heads or bushy materials, yet will just as easily cut through a finger-thick branch. The colour makes them easy to find amid the greenery.

BUCKETS AND CANS

One tall and one short bucket will be needed at the start. These can be ordinary household buckets with a swing handle, but graduate to proper *flower buckets* with side handles if you can. Flower heads are less likely to be trapped and damaged in these.

A *long-spouted can* (**7**) – the type used for watering house-plants – is necessary for topping up water in containers. Cans usually hold about 0.5 litre (1 pint). In an emergency a teapot with a spout is a good substitute.

TAPES

There are two sorts of tape used in flower arranging, each for a very different purpose:

Thick sticky tape (**10**), in green or white, 5 mm (¼ in) and 12 mm (½ in) wide, is used for strapping foam or wire into containers, strapping sticks on to candles, etc.

Stem-binding tape (**9**) is thinner, 12 mm (½ in) wide, in green, brown or white. It is used for binding wire and false stems. Of plastic or waxed crepe paper, it stretches very slightly and will stick to itself when warm and pressed in the hand.

WIRES

Reel wire (**14**) is a fairly fine wire with many uses, such as tying down crumpled mesh into a container, securing a container to a stand and wiring dried flowers and leaves.

Rose wires (**29, 30**) are fine, silvery wires for delicate floristry or artificial-flower work. They range from 0.38 mm (fine) to 0.28 mm (very fine) in thickness and are 180 mm (7 in) long.

Stub wires (**28**) are used for false stems of dried and preserved flowers, leaves and cones, for strengthening fresh stems and for a hundred odd uses. They are made in various lengths, from 130 mm (5 in) to 460 mm (18 in), and in different thicknesses. The most popular for general use is a medium 0.71 mm which used to be, and often still is, called 22-gauge.

Wire coat hangers pulled into a roughly circular shape make a good basis for circular wreaths.

STICKS

A bundle of *kebab sticks* (**27**) and *cocktail sticks/toothpicks* (**12**) should be in every arranger's workbox. They are useful for strengthening stems, providing false stems, fixing fruits and candles, applying spots of glue, making holes in floral foam for soft-stemmed flowers such as daffodils, and piercing clingfilm when it is used in making garlands.

POLYTHENE

Two *sheets of thick polythene* are invaluable, one to work on and one to put on the floor. Thick newspaper will serve instead.

Polythene bags in different sizes, with wire twists, are useful for transporting leaves, storing containers to keep them dust free and holding rubbish.

Cling film in rolls for the kitchen, can be used to wrap floral foam to conserve moisture, especially for garlands and swags that cannot be watered once they are in place.

A roll of *rubbish bags* is handy to take along whenever you make an arrangement away from home, to dispose of cut-off stalks, leaves and broken flower heads.

TYING MATERIALS

A reel of *green garden twine* (**11**) and a bundle of *raffia* (**5, 20**) have many uses in tying bunches for transportation. A small *ball of wool* is handy for tying rosebuds gently closed to delay their opening.

TOOLS

Sooner or later you will find the following almost essential: *thorn strippers* (**18**), *pliers* (**24**), a *screwdriver* (**25**), an old *kitchen knife* (**22**) for cutting foam, a metal *skewer* (**23**), and *wire cutters* (pictured on pages 76 and 80). A *glue gun*, an *electric drill* and a *folding saw* are useful luxuries.

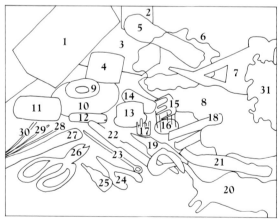

1 Floral foam block
2 Floral foam round
3 Dry foam block
4 Floral foam round
5 Raffia
6 5 cm (2 in) wire mesh
7 Long-spouted can
8 Towel
9 Stem binding
10 Sticky tape
11 Garden twine
12 Cocktail sticks/ toothpicks
13 Metal pinholder
14 Reel wire
15 Plastic foam holder ('frog')
16 Metal foam holder (anchor)
17 Plastic foam holder ('frog')
18 Thorn strippers
19 Secateurs
20 Raffia
21 Putty-type adhesive
22 Knife
23 Metal skewer
24 Pliers
25 Screwdriver
26 Flower scissors
27 Kebab sticks
28 Green coated stub wires
29 Rose wires
30 Rose wires
31 Plastic mesh

Containers

Don't rush out to buy expensive containers before you have some experience. There is generally some household item which will serve well enough for the time being at least.

Look at the contents of kitchen or china cabinets with new eyes. Tall vases and glass receptacles of any kind, out of fashion for many years, are now popular again, so search out grandmother's vase or rose-bowl if you still have them.

CONTAINER	HOW TO USE
Jug or vase	For simple, no-mechanics arrangements or with crumpled mesh.
Low bowl, casserole dish, vegetable tureen	For use with pinholder, crumpled mesh, a combination of the two, or floral foam.
Basket	Many shapes and sizes can be used. So it will hold water, a liner is needed, such as a plastic box, food tin, plant-pot saucer or basin.
Box such as a writing box, jewel case, cigar box, or cutlery canteen	Needs a liner, possibly a plastic box cut down with scissors.
Candlestick or candelabra	To hold a round of foam, fit it with a candlecup in plastic or metal to suit the holder, painting the cup if necessary.
Wine bottle	Fit with candlecup as for candlestick and use a round of floral foam.
Tins, such as sardine, baked-bean, ham, pie or loaf tins	Collect a few and paint or spray them black, grey or dark green.

EARLY INEXPENSIVE BUYS

Small plastic and ceramic dishes made to hold a round of floral foam can be bought in garden centres, floral accessory departments and florists.

A plastic plant-pot saucer and flower pot (upturned) glued together, then painted, will make a container similar to the one on pages 18–19.

Plastic urns can be found in different sizes and proportions, with and without handles and plinths, at garden centres (where they are sold for patio use), hardware shops, florists and often in street markets, car boot sales and garage sales. Not only are plastic urns inexpensive, but they have the advantage of being lightweight (and therefore easily portable) and also unbreakable.

Reject china and glassware shops often have well-shaped bowls, jars and vases. Consider painting or spraying them to suit your own colour schemes.

Mechanics

The term 'mechanics' refers to the device(s) used to support the stems in an arrangement. The photograph opposite shows some examples.

A *pinholder* (13) has close-set pins in a weighty lead base. A *foam holder* (16) is similar to a pinholder but has about eight long pins set in a lead base. 'Frogs' (15, 17) are cheap plastic, expendable foam holders; they come in two sizes.

Plasticine is sometimes used for securing pinholders and foam holders, but *putty-type adhesive* (21), which comes as a green strip on a roll with paper backing, is preferred as it is more reliable than plasticine. It is needed, either in strips or round blobs, to secure pinholders and foam holders to a *dry* container. Dryness is essential. It simply does not work otherwise.

Water-retaining floral foam, sold under the tradenames Oasis and Bloomfix, is a green foam that absorbs many times its own weight in water. It is available in a variety of shapes and sizes, but the most useful are blocks (1) measuring $23 \times 11 \times 8$ cm ($9 \times 4\frac{1}{2} \times 3$ in) and rounds (2, 4) measuring 6 cm ($2\frac{1}{2}$ in) in thickness and 8 cm (3 in) in diameter. Foam can be cut to size before or after soaking. Fill a large basin or washing-up bowl with water and put the foam on top. It will sink slowly to the water level in one or two minutes, which means it has absorbed as much water as it can hold. Remove it immediately from the water, and use. Even when using soaked foam, fill the container with water to within 1.5 cm ($\frac{1}{2}$ in) of the top and top up to this level daily.

Dry foam (3) comes in brown or beige blocks and rounds the same sizes as green foam. It does not hold water and is used for dried or artificial stems.

Wire mesh (6), sometimes called chicken wire, in a 5 cm (2 in) gauge can be crumpled to make several layers of holes to support stems. Cut off the thick selvedge before using it. Wire mesh in a 2.5 cm (1 in) gauge is used to cover foam to give extra support for large arrangements, garlands and swags. *Plastic mesh* (31) can be used as a substitute for wire mesh; it is best in deep jugs and other containers.

If you don't have any of the above to hand, you can use sand, gravel, crumpled newspaper, cellophane tape criss-crossed over the mouth of the container or cut stems packed vertically.

In glass containers you can use broken windshield glass, glass marbles or nuggets packed into the container, or crystals that make an aqueous gel when mixed with water. These are sold as Crystal Earth, Crystal Soil (in the United States) or Magic Mulch.

The picture below shows several containers already fitted with various mechanics. Of course, not all containers need special mechanics: everyday jugs (1, 3, 6, 9, 11), for example, are excellent just as they are, for simple bunches of mixed or one-type flowers.

A brass candlestick (2) has been fitted with a brass candlecup ready to take a round of foam.

An inexpensive plastic urn (4) holds a block of foam protruding well above the container, strapped in with white sticky tape.

A shallow plastic plant-pot saucer (5) has crumpled wire mesh domed up above the container and well secured with crossed-over bands of green sticky tape.

The ceramic dish (7) is one of the many inexpensive ceramic dishes designed to hold a round of foam.

The glass vase (8) has glass marbles to hold flower stems in place.

The decorative wire basket (10) could be used with a liner to hold water.

1 Jug
2 Candlestick with candlecup for foam
3 Jug
4 Plastic urn with foam
5 Plant-pot saucer with wire mesh
6 Jug
7 Ceramic dish with foam
8 Glass vase and marbles
9 Jug
10 Wire basket
11 Jug

Cutting or Buying

The care you take in these preliminary stages will make all the difference to both the appearance and the life of a flower arrangement.

CUTTING

● If you can, cut plant material in the cool part of the day (early morning or late evening).
● Cut with scissors, secateurs or a sharp knife (rather than picking with the fingers) to make a clean severance with the least damage to the stem or the plant.
● Cut stems with consideration for the shape of the plant, not all from one side, top or bottom. This is especially important with young shrubs and trees.

BUYING

● Most *bulb flowers and roses* (daffodils, narcissi, tulips, iris, anemones, roses) should be bought in bud, but with some petal colour showing, otherwise they may not open at all.
● *Daisy-type flowers* (gerberas, marguerites, chrysanthemums) should have tight centres that are greenish in colour, rather than deep yellow which shows the pollen is ripe and the flower's life half over. Petals should not be dropping.
● *Spikes* (gladioli, delphiniums, freesias and blossom) should have only three or four of the lower florets open.
● *Carnations*, if single blooms, should be almost fully open, but with no white 'threads' showing or they are too mature; the smaller, spray type should have about one-third of the florets open.
● *Stems and leaves* of all purchases should be examined. Leaves should be crisp and green, not discoloured, while stems should be firm and not slimy or brown at the ends.
● All *flowers and leaves* should be put into water as soon as possible.

Conditioning

This is the term used by flower arrangers to describe the preparation of flowers and leaves *before* arranging them. Conditioning helps to make them last longer and keeps them in better condition throughout what the commercial sellers call their 'vase life'.

When leaves and flowers are cut, their water supply from the roots is cut off at once and many will wilt in a short time. If they are put into water quickly, they will soon revive, but as this is not always possible, it is sensible to get into a good routine for dealing with cut plant material as soon as you get home.

1 · Fill one or two buckets approximately two-thirds full of clean water.

2 · Re-cut all stems on a slant. It is enough to remove even less than 1 cm (½ in).

3 · If stems are thick or woody, slit the ends for about 2.5 cm (1 in) and scrape away the bark from about 2.5–5 cm (1–2 in).

4 · Trim away any thorns, snags, low side-shoots and leaves that will be under water, for ease of handling and more space in the bucket.

5 · Put stems into the water at once and leave them in a cool place for an hour or two, or overnight if possible, before arranging them.

6 · It is still debatable whether vase-life is prolonged by adding a proprietary compound (such as Chrysal) to the conditioning water and to the water in the vase. Scientific evidence regarding it is scarce, but you may wish to do so. If you prefer to try a home-made solution, dissolve 15 ml (1 tablespoon) of sugar and 5 ml (1 teaspoon) of household bleach in 0.5 litre (1 pint) of water.

7·Single leaves (except grey ones) and small sprays should be submerged under water for at least an hour or two to become fully charged with water. Very young leaves picked in spring before they have matured can be submerged, perhaps for an hour, but the tips, at least, will turn brown if submerged for too long. Larger sprays of leaves that are impractical to submerge (unless a bath is free for long enough!) should stand in deep water and be mist-sprayed as often as possible.

SPECIAL TREATMENTS

Even with this care some flower heads or leaves will still be limp. There are several ways of tackling this.

Singeing: Any stem which exudes milky latex when cut should be singed in a candle flame before being given its long drink. Hold the stem end in a flame until it is charred and the latex stops running, then put it in water. Poppies, spurges and poinsettias benefit from this.

Re-cutting stems under water: This is always practised in ikebana (Japanese arranging). It requires a wide bowl of water, so that the actual re-cutting takes place under water to eliminate the possibility of an air-lock in the stem. They should be put immediately into deep water for a long drink.

Boiling stem ends: This ruthless-sounding operation is wholly beneficial and will revive leaf sprays that have wilted and flower heads that have drooped or

bent over at the neck, as bought roses sometimes do. The effect is magical, and if flowers and leaves have to last a long time at a show, exhibition or church festival it is well worth giving this treatment *before* they are given a long drink. Bring a few inches of water to boil in an old saucepan. Meanwhile wrap the flower heads and leaves in a towel or cloth to protect them

from the steam and hold about 5 cm (2 in) of the stem in the boiling water for about 30 seconds. Then give the usual long, deep drink.

De-foliating: Some cut stems – including lilac, mock-orange blossom (philadelphus) and laburnum – just cannot take up water fast enough to support both flower heads and leaves. Consequently, they need to be stripped of leaves completely. Other shrub flowers, such as hydrangeas and weigela, will benefit from having leaves thinned out.

Floating: Sometimes it helps to revive wilted flowers if they are floated on water for an hour or so.

A Bunch in a Jug

A bunch of flowers in a jug or vase of water is the simplest form of flower arranging. It adds colour and often scent to a room and provides a living finishing touch. The bouquet here is a colourful mix of flowers from a spring garden and the florist's shop. You could also use a couple of cheap market bunches of one kind of flower, a birthday bouquet or sprays of leaves and berries in their autumn colours.

OVERALL SIZE (W × H)
90 × 100 cm (36 × 40 in)

YOU WILL NEED
Stoneware pitcher 30 cm (12 in) high

PLANT MATERIAL
10 each tulips and daffodils
5 iris
7 stems forsythia
5 stems pussy willow (Salix caprea)
5 stems winter honeysuckle (Lonicera fragrantissima)
A few hellebores

ARRANGER
Margaret McSheehy

1 · Condition spring flowers well, especially if from florist. Fill the container two-thirds full of water.

2 · To assess where to cut the first stem, hold it upside-down outside the container with the tip resting against the table or floor where the flowers will stand, then cut the stem at the point where you feel the top of the arrangement should be. For good proportion the stems should be cut at least two and a half to three times the container height. (Remember, one-third will go down into the container and not be seen, leaving one and a half to twice the height above the container.) You can always cut off another inch or so if necessary.

3 · Put this stem in the water and add several others cut a little shorter. Remember to cut on the slant and to slit woody stems. At this stage they will move about, but as more stems go in they will support each other. The tallest can then be steadied centrally at the back of the pitcher.

4 · Continue adding stems, cutting them at different lengths (but none taller than the original 'backbone' stem), with some short enough to reach only just above the container rim. Keep the larger flowers towards the middle of the arrangement.

5 · Try not to have all the flowers facing towards the front. Turn some to the side and even to the back to show different aspects and to create depth. For the same reason place some flowers towards the back. When finished the arrangement should be almost as wide from front to back as it is from side to side.

6 · Mix colours and shapes so that there are some of each kind of flower to the left and right of the centre tallest stem. This will give a symmetry to the group and a sense of balance.

7 · When enough stems have been put in to give stability to the arrangement, survey the result and shorten one or two stems if flower heads are crowding each other. See that some flower heads or leaves come over the rim of the jug to break the hard line. Fill the jug to within 2 cm (¾ in) of the top using a long-spouted watering can.

Checking the Arrangement

● The finished arrangement has a roughly triangular outline but its composition is apparently casual. The emphasis is on colour and shape and achieving a fairly symmetrical balance about the central stem.
● Long, slender plant material (forsythia, pussy willow and winter honeysuckle) makes the outline, with the blue iris and yellow tulips bringing the eye down to where the red tulips and large daffodils focus attention near the container rim.
● Because all the stems radiate from the jug a natural rhythm is created which helps to unite the bunch into a pleasing whole.

Other Options

This type of arrangement without mechanics can be in any container that is taller than it is wide, from a small milk or cream jug to a large pottery vase. Keep a sense of proportion between the size of the container and the size of the flowers or leaves put in it. Full-blown roses or large dahlias look wrong in a small container, just as forget-me-nots and primroses are dwarfed by a tall one.

Bunches of one type of flower, whether from garden, shop or market look good in a vase or jug that picks up the colour of the flowers (or vice-versa). Two or three bunches of inexpensive daffodils look marvellous in a brown jug. An arrangement of

leaves may not be thought of as colourful, but there is a surprising range if you look carefully. There are greys and limes, reds and purples and all sorts of variegations in yellow and white.

The picture on page 5, arranged by *Liz Hunter-Craig*, shows a similar treatment. A cottagey mixed bunch of flowers from an autumn garden is arranged simply in a blue glass vase. The larger blue flowers are monkshood (aconitum) and there is golden rod, astrantia, polygonum, rose-hips, abelia and sedum, with snowberries showing up clearly in front of the vase.

A Vertical Design

A complete contrast from the simple, unstructured arrangement of many flowers in a jug shown on page 17, this tall, slender arrangement requires the support of 'mechanics' to keep it in place. Very little plant material is used and only three different kinds. All the stems are held on a pinholder in the shallow bowl at the top of the container.

OVERALL SIZE (W×H)
20×75 cm (8×30 in)

YOU WILL NEED
Raised ceramic container about 20 cm (8 in) high
Piece of slate (optional)

MECHANICS
Pinholder 7.5 cm (3 in) in diameter
Putty-type adhesive

PLANT MATERIAL
2 leaves New Zealand flax about 60 cm (24 in)
3 stems gladioli
6–7 hosta leaves

ARRANGER
Ruth Ledder

To emphasize the vertical quality of this design, height is exaggerated. The tallest leaf is nearly four times the height of the container and base.

The pinholder, or needlepoint holder, came to the West from Japan, where it is known as a *kenzan*. It is the basis of many Japanese arrangements, or ikebana. The sharp pins are closely set in a heavy lead base, which gives it stability. The Japanese do not fix the pinholder in the container, but Western arrangers secure it with several small pieces of putty-type adhesive.

1 · Fix the pinholder in the *dry* container with three or four pills of putty-type adhesive. A firm clockwise twist, as if you are tightening a screw-top jar, will make sure that the pinholder is quite securely in place. Now put the container in position, on a base if you wish.

2 · Cut the New Zealand flax leaves on the slant, one taller than the other. Press them on to the pins at the back of the pinholder. Be sure that they are upright.

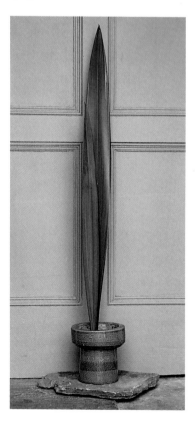

3 · Add a stem of gladiolus that has buds at the top, immediately in front of the tallest leaf and a few inches shorter. A second gladiolus is added, a little to the left and shorter still. The third needs flowers fairly wide open. Cut the stem so that the lowest flower is about 7.5 cm (3 in) above the rim of the vase. Reduce the thickness of the flower stems by removing any leaves and cutting on a slant.

4 · Now add the hosta leaves to give more width and visual weight at the bottom of the design. Here, one leaf, a little to the left, is quite tall: the others should have stems of varying lengths and at least one should curve over the container rim, to break the hard line. Try to avoid the effect of a regular frill. When adding these leaves it is best to push each stem firmly and vertically down on to the pins, then gently ease it to the slanting angle you want. Add water almost to the top of the container.

Checking the Arrangement

● This very tailored and controlled vertical structure is an important basis on which a number of other arrangements can be built. The 'backbone', or first stem, of *any* arrangement needs to be upright like this; otherwise the subsequent stems will all begin to list to one side or tilt forward.

● It also illustrates how important it is to place this first stem well back in the container, whatever mechanics are being used, so that you don't run out of space and support at the front. Be sure to make use of the whole pinholder.

● The success of this type of arrangement lies in its elegant proportions and the choice of three very different types of plant material, which complement each other in shape and colouring. The coral-coloured gladioli pick up the red edges of the New Zealand flax (this variety is 'Maori Sunset'), while the broader triangular shape of the hosta leaves gives a pleasing contrast to the rounder forms of the open gladioli flowers.

Other Options

Many variations are possible, including the use of other blade-shaped leaves such as iris or yucca. For the tallest placements there are also bulrushes/reedmace, spikes of delphinium, larkspur or monkshood (aconitum) or stems of pussy willow (*Salix caprea*). Instead of the three gladioli, consider using five or seven roses, tulips, daffodils or dahlias. If these are graded down from buds at the top to wide open flowers near the container rim, the same effect will be achieved. As a substitute for the hosta leaves, you could try using bergenia, arum, heuchera, fatshedera, large ivy or spotted laurel (aucuba).

A Christmas Table

The traditional colours of red and green with touches of white and gold are always the most popular for Christmas arrangements. The low arrangement shown here is useful to have on the table during the day or as a centrepiece for Christmas dinner, and it can easily be adapted to suit the shape of the table. For safety's sake, plant material near the candle is kept low so that it will be well away from the flame.

OVERALL SIZE (W × H)
60 × 30 cm (24 × 12 in)

YOU WILL NEED
Small gold dish raised a little on feet or on a plinth
30 cm (12 in) red candle

MECHANICS
Block of soaked floral foam
Green sticky tape
Candleholder or cocktail sticks (used on page 36)

PLANT MATERIAL
6 pieces rosemary
6 pieces lime-green cupressus
A few variegated ivy leaves
Sprigs of laurustinus in flower
8 stems variegated holly
6 pieces plain green holly
8 poppy seedheads painted/ sprayed gold
5 stems red spray carnations
10 single-bloom red carnations

ARRANGER
Mary Napper

1 · If you can, work *in situ*, because the lighting angle and colour links will be easier to see, but protect the dining table with a thick sheet of polythene. Set the container in place so that you can judge the necessary length and width of the arrangement.

2 · Secure the soaked block of foam with green sticky tape. Here it has been taken across the foam diagonally with the ends meeting under the dish. One strap will be enough as there is no tall plant material, only the central candle. Put the candle in its plastic holder in the centre of the block of foam.

3 · Decide what length and width you would like the arrangement to be and establish this with stems of rosemary pushed into the *sides* of the foam low down near the dish.

4 · Add some cupressus and ivy to start covering the mechanics and position a sprig of laurustinus to mark the height. Keep plant material low by the candle so that it can be lit and burn safely. Continue putting most of the stems into the *sides* of the foam, with the longer pieces of holly filling out the length.

5 · It is usually better to remove all the holly leaves from the stems that have the best berries because they will show up better. Sprays of leaves can go in separately. (If berries are scarce, it is worth buying artificial ones and wiring them into clusters with a false wire stem. Tucked in among the leaves the berries will look very realistic.)

6 · Add the gold poppy seedheads which will catch the light and give a rich look.

7 · Add the flowers last, having created a framework of green and gold for them. Cut the spray carnations so that you have several longer stems with half-open buds to reach almost to the tips of the rosemary stems put in first. Use the shorter stems of flowers that are more fully open, all around the arrangement. Sit down at the table while doing this and you will see it from the angle of the seated diners, so you can fill in any gaps and make any necessary adjustments. Keep the large carnations nearer the centre in order to focus attention near the candle.

8 · Remove the polythene sheet and set the arrangement on a table centre or base. Check that there is no plant material too near the candle, and remember never to leave it burning unattended. If it isn't to be lit until later, trim the wick neatly and see that it is upright, not drooping.

Checking the Arrangement

● If the table is round, the shape can easily be adjusted to suit. In that case establish the outline with three equally spaced pieces of rosemary (imagine a clock face and put them at 4, 8 and 12 o'clock), followed by holly, cupressus, etc.
● If the table is a long one, a small posy arrangement at each end will have the effect of taking the decoration down the full length.
● As a table arrangement will be near food and close to seated diners, all foliage must be scrupulously clean.

Other Options

The long, low arrangement is one of the most popular table decorations and can be used at any time of year. Fresh yellow flowers can enliven similar evergreens in early spring. In summer lighter foliages and multicoloured flowers are pretty, or white and green look fresh and cool. Autumn berries and dahlias look good with orange, yellow or gold candles. Use two or three candles inserted in the foam block to make a variation. Dried and preserved leaves and seedheads with a few fresh flowers are effective

with toning candles and napkins. At Christmas time, artificial plant materials are usually acceptable. Plastic, fabric and paper flowers are so good nowadays, that when arranged with natural evergreens, they are almost undetectable from the real thing. Artificial carnations, roses and poinsettias are especially effective. Gold, silver and white plastic leaves can be used to lighten dark evergreens, or for one-colour arrangements that are wholly artificial. Glittering coloured baubles and artificial fruits, realistic or frankly fake, can add colour and useful round shapes.

PARALLELS IN A TROUGH

In recent years there has been much interest in what has come to be called the 'parallel' or 'European continental' style of arranging. Unlike traditional arranging, stems do not radiate from a central point, but stand up vertically, or are layered horizontally. The style originated with florists in Europe, especially in Holland. Inspired by the straight stems, uniform size of blooms and large patches of colour in the flower markets, they used blocks of one-type, one-colour flowers, leaves or stems springing up from a groundwork, or patchwork, of tightly packed short-stemmed flowers, leaves, moss and fruits.

OVERALL SIZE (W × H)
53 × 50 cm (21 × 20 in)

YOU WILL NEED
Trough or lined basket
40 × 10 cm (16 × 4 in)

MECHANICS
2 blocks floral foam cut to fit and protruding 4 cm (1½ in) above rim
2 large 'frogs'
Putty-type adhesive

PLANT MATERIAL
3 stems Leycesteria formosa
3 stems globe thistle
6–7 stems Clematis tangutica
8 leaves of scented geranium
3 white tulips
3 white eustoma
4 houseleeks (sempervivum)
5 leaves each arum and houttuynia
1 white hydrangea flower
1 stem green Chinese lanterns (physalis)
7 ivy flowers
5 black-eyed susans
5 yellow rosebuds
5 ferns

ARRANGER
Kare Tarr

Beginners often find this an easy style because the groupings can look very pleasing without much practice. Although such an apparently simple arrangement takes a surprising quantity of plant material, much of it can be easy to get and inexpensive. Dried can be mixed with fresh, and fruit and vegetables can be used for the groundwork.

1 · Cut the foam to size and soak it for no more than about a minute and a half. Take two large-sized 'frogs' and put three pills of putty-type adhesive underneath each. Make sure everything is *dry*, including the inside of the container. Press them down and give them a slight twist (like tightening a screw lid) to make sure they are secure. Push the blocks of foam on to the 'frogs'. Before starting to arrange, chamfer the edges of the foam.

2 · Insert the leycesteria stems in a close group at the back left of the foam. Make sure they are vertical. Do the same with the thistles on the back right corner of the foam. They should be about two-thirds of the height of the other stems. The yellow clematis flowers similarly go in as a tight bunch, left and forward of the thistles.

3 · Build up a layer of variegated geranium leaves on the right front corner of the arrangement. Put the longest stems into the side of the foam and the shorter ones on top of the foam.

4 · Add white tulips and eustoma on the left. Insert houseleeks so that they come down over the front of the container, and layer arum leaves over the corner and side. Add florets of white hydrangea as a central group and Chinese lanterns, to strengthen the globe thistle stems.

5 · More yellow is introduced with fluffy ivy flowers on the left, black-eyed susans behind the tulip stems and a row of yellow rosebuds next to the white hydrangea.

6 · The groundwork is finished off with variegated houttuynia leaves and a few ferns at the back right.

Checking the Arrangement

● The aim throughout when arranging in this style should be to seek out stems that are as straight as possible for the verticals. To assist in this, stems are sometimes bunched together and tied, or held by a rubber band, just under the flower heads and again at the ends of the stems. They may even be tied decoratively – the term is 'bundling' – with string, raffia, ribbon, cord or tape in all sorts of ways including cross-gartering.
● In both the verticals and the short-stemmed groundwork,

blocks and patches of different colours, shapes and textures are deliberately placed next to each other to point up the contrast. There is no gentle transition.
● There must be repetition of colour or shape in the arrangement to give some rhythm to it. Look how white is taken through the design. Yellow is repeated in the roses, clematis and black-eyed susans, but the shapes are different. The balls of the thistles find an echo in the ivy flowers, yet the textures are different. The leaves at the two front corners are both variegated and trangular, but again the texture is different.

Other Options

There is really no limit to the choice of plant material in any season. Fruits and vegetables are very often included in the ground-work (eg apples, tangerines, Brussels sprouts, mushrooms, calabrese) speared on cocktail sticks/toothpicks inserted into the foam. Bundles of cut stalks and candles may be included in the verticals and perhaps just one curving branch of contorted willow or hazel to add an element of surprise.

A much larger version of parallels is on pages 152–3.

CREATING A LANDSCAPE

A landscape arrangement aims to create a natural scene and is really a development of the moss gardens many people must remember having made in childhood. An attractive branch is chosen to represent a tree, with flowers and leaves that might grow naturally beside it. The addition of a model bird and its nest increases the interest and tells a little story. The scene can suggest a meadow, woodland, riverside, seashore, lake, moorland or garden.

OVERALL SIZE (W×H)
50×75 cm (20×30 in)

YOU WILL NEED
Flat piece of wood or slate or an oval piece of hardboard covered with natural hessian (burlap)
2 small tins or ceramic dishes in an earthy colour
Small pill bottle
2 pieces of stone or slate
Chunky piece of natural wood

MECHANICS
2 pinholders
Crumpled wire mesh
Putty-type adhesive

PLANT MATERIAL
Curving branch, bare or with buds
Moss, arum and ivy leaves, 3 ferns
Small conifer branch (cupressus)
Daffodils
Small spring flowers
Echeveria or houseleeks (sempervivum)

ACCESSORIES
Model bird
Small nest (bought or found deserted)
Sugar/plastic birds' eggs

ARRANGER
Anne Blunt

1 · Place the base at a slight angle on the table/shelf where the arrangement will stand. (It is always better to work *in situ* whenever possible.) Position the main container about one-third of the way along the base. This is where the tallest stem will be. Secure a pinholder in it with putty-type adhesive and crumple a small piece of wire mesh over it.

2 · Choosing and placing the main branch is important because it establishes the overall height and its curve will form a frame for the picture being created. Budding branches are especially effective since the tiny new leaves are in scale. Look for a branch with a strong, pleasantly curved line.

Cut away any side shoots that confuse or spoil the line. Trim them close to the main branch and rub the cut(s) with dirt or with a pencil to disguise the new scar. Place the branch in the pinholder then add slate around the base.

3 · Add some moss around the stones. To begin to build up the groundwork and mask the mechanics, put in several larger leaves at different angles and with stems of different lengths. Add a few ferns and put the conifer branch in a dish with a small pinholder on the left behind the slate pieces. Tuck echeveria or houseleeks under the stones in front.

4 · Add the daffodils and a few of their own leaves in a cluster at the foot of the tree. Put the other flowers with two or three of their own leaves in the little bottle with water.

5 · Adding accessories is by no means essential and the arrangement can be complete at this stage. However, the bird is appealing and adds another dimension to the story. Tuck the nest in front of the container. Most model birds have wires already attached to their feet for fixing to a perch, but if this is not the case, twist a

length of reel wire around the feet to attach the bird to an appropriate stone or branch. A few confectionery or plastic eggs in the nest will complete the scene.

Checking the Arrangement

● Scale, the size relationship between different items in a design, is important here; a flower that is too large can soon destroy the illusion. Smaller rather than larger daffodils, for example, will suit the arrangement better. (More about scale in Chapter 3.)
● Seasons also play an important part in establishing the illusion. Chrysanthemums, for example, which are florist's flowers obtainable all year round, do not truly suggest spring because they would not be flowering outdoors in that season. In the same way flowers from more exotic climates, such as orchids, anthuriums or strelitzias, will not look at home in a spring meadow.
● Check the balance of the tallest stem in this arrangement. Although curved, it must look essentially upright or the whole arrangement will seem to be falling over to one side.

Other Options

Landscape scenes can be created in a similar way at other times of the year. In winter a bare branch, touched with artificial snow or painted white, can be arranged with ivy, berried holly, other evergreens and fir or pine cones. Autumn leaves, berried branches and seedheads are also effective, and a holiday may provide the ingredients for a seashore scene.

Garden landscape arrangements can be recreated with cultivated flowers and shrubs. Urban-style landscapes have recently become popular, featuring 'architectural' arrangements on a base of gravel or paving stone, with small-scale columns or statuary.

CHAPTER ONE · REVIEW

*T*his first chapter has concentrated on introducing you to the basics of flower arranging. No matter how simple the arrangement, it will benefit from the use of the right cutting and conditioning techniques and the most suitable tools, equipment and mechanics. You don't need a great deal to start out with – it's better to add to your collection of containers and equipment gradually when you are sure what you want.

Mechanics

Three different types of mechanics have been introduced:
● a pinholder
● green floral foam which holds many times its weight in water
● crumpled wire mesh/chicken wire
We have also used three different ways of fixing them in a container:
● putty-type adhesive
● green sticky tape
● plastic foam holders known as 'frogs'
With only a few exceptions these mechanics are used, alone or in combination, for every arrangement, large or small, in the entire course.

Time is never wasted in making sure the mechanics are firm and secure and are suitable for the type and size of arrangement they are to hold.

Styles

The chapter has introduced five styles of arrangement. The first may have been familiar, while the others may be new. Between them they form the basis of most of the designs in this book:
● The bunch in the jug is always with us. Simple and quick, colourful and unsophisticated, it is right anywhere: on a hall table, desk, kitchen table or dresser, window sill or bedside cupboard, or as a floor-standing corner-piece.

● The tall, slim vertical, so useful in a space where width is restricted, is also the 'backbone' and central framework of most triangular and fan-shaped arrangements.
● The low table arrangement, surprisingly enough, is based on a horizontal version of the slim vertical. Tapering points, with bushier material in between, lead the eye to larger, rounded forms at the centre of the arrangement.
● The parallels are very much a late 20th century style and have given a new dimension to flower arranging.
● The landscape is an inexpensive decoration and because it can be evocative of a particular place and season has many possibilities when it comes to interpretative arranging (see Chapter 8).

Accessories

Non-plant materials have also been introduced because arrangements often gain by having accessories added. Candles are the arrangers' most popular accessory for table decoration, even though today they are seldom relied on entirely for lighting.

The bird which is used in the landscape scene gives added appeal and another dimension to the 'story' the landscape tells, but it is important that any accessory should appear to be in scale with the plant materials used.

Choosing Plant Material

Remember that a flower arranger uses more than just flowers and leaves. There are also seedheads, grasses, bare stems, berries, fruit, cones, vegetables, moss, lichen, fungi, bark, wood, nuts, succulents, spathes, catkins, cereal plants, reeds and rushes. Check through and see how many of these have been used in the first five arrangements.

For the beginner, knowing what to pick or what to

buy is often one of the greatest difficulties. Like learning to drive, there seem to be so many things to think about and so many actions to take at the same time!

Look back at the arrangements in this chapter and notice how each of them uses three basic shapes of plant material:

Outline material is long-stemmed, fairly narrow, often pointed; it is quite often foliage, unopened or part-open buds, sprays of blossoms, spikes of flowers or slender branches. Examples used are forsythia, New Zealand flax, pussy willow, gladioli, rosemary, spray carnation buds and budding branches.

Intermediate and bushy, sometimes called 'transition' material, includes clusters of leaves or flowers; half-open flowers; bushy sprays. Examples used are iris, hellebores, holly, laurustinus, cupressus, ferns, snowdrops, sedum, and abelia.

Rounded shapes, often called focal 'points', include fully open flowers; larger leaves, rounded, triangular or oval in shape; cones; fruits and berry clusters. Examples used are tulips, open gladiolus flowers, hosta leaves, carnations, holly-berry clusters, hydrangeas, roses, daffodils, echeveria, large ivy leaves and arum leaves.

Arrangements for Your Own Home

Any of these five arrangements may fit into your home. Take stock of the places where they could stand, for each one is essentially a different shape and needs a different setting.

Note the colours of your furnishings in each room. Which colour flowers look best with them? Do you have containers of suitable colour or would you consider painting or spraying any of them (*not* the best china) to fit in better?

Chapter Two

MORE ABOUT DESIGN

While many people arrange flowers pleasingly without ever actually thinking about design, an understanding of design principles and elements helps in choosing plant materials for a particular container or style of arrangement. Not everyone has an instinctive flair for putting the best colours or shapes or textures together, but everyone can learn more about them and so make more informed choices. This chapter deals with the elements of design: colour, form (or shape), line, texture and space. The principles of design are covered in Chapter 3.

The elements of design are the physical qualities that every object and piece of plant material possesses. Everything has a colour and a shape we can see, a texture we can see and feel, and space around it and even within it (as in a trumpet-shaped flower, for example) which we do not always find easy to see and appreciate.

Colour

Whereas the painter has to make his colours from pigments, the arranger generally works with the colours that already exist in plant material, and is concerned with selecting and composing them rather than actually creating them.

THE ARTIST'S PIGMENT THEORY

There are a number of colour theories and terminologies, so flower arrangers use the one that is most convenient: the artist's pigment theory, based on the mixing of paint.

Briefly the pigment theory is based on three *primary* colours – red, yellow and blue – and three *secondary* colours, made by mixing the primaries. Thus, orange is made by mixing red and yellow, green from yellow and blue, and purple (or violet) from blue and red. There is an infinite range of variation between them.

The six hues can be set out as a colour wheel showing colour relationships and variations from light to dark. This colour wheel is shown on page 30. Red comes opposite green, yellow opposite purple and blue opposite orange – in other words, the primary is opposite the secondary colour made by the other two primaries. Colours opposite each other on the colour wheel are known as *complementary* colours.

Pale colours are called *tints* because white has been added to the main hue. Red with white makes pink, yellow with white makes cream, and so on.

Dark colours are created by adding black and are called *shades*: blue with black makes navy blue, green with black makes dark pine green, etc. Notice, however that orange with black makes brown.

Grey (ie black and white) added to any colour produces a greyed *tone*, though the term 'tone' is generally used to mean *any* colour deviating from the pure hue, whether tone, tint or shade.

LUMINOSITY

The other aspect of colour that is important to arrangers is the quality known as *luminosity*, which is its capacity to show up in poor light.

The most luminous colours are the tints – those with a good deal of white in them (ie those we normally refer to as pastels) – as well as white itself, red, yellow, orange and yellow-green.

Form and Shape

Although 'shape' is often considered to be two-dimensional and 'form' three-dimensional, the terms are used interchangeably here.

Plant material may be grouped into three categories of shape (outline, intermediate and rounded), as already discussed in Chapter 1, but the actual variations within these groups are enormous. There are at least 30 *named* leaf shapes, each of which can vary not only in size but also in colour. Flower formations are equally diverse, and when all the other types of plant material are added, the arranger has theoretically hundreds to choose from (though only one or two may be available at any one time!).

Most arrangements need variety of form to give interest to the design, but they also need to have some forms repeated, though perhaps in a different colour or texture.

Line

Line is truly a variation and extended version of shape, but worth treating separately as it plays such an important part in many arrangements, particularly in parallel and freestyle designs.

Line can be straight, gently curving, swirling, zig-zag or criss-crossed. It can be thick or thin; horizontal, vertical or diagonal; continuous or broken. It gives direction, movement and rhythm to the design, leading the eye from one part to another in a continuous or an interrupted sequence.

Texture

Texture is the surface quality of an object. It can be both seen and touched. The arranger is mainly concerned with the effect of visual texture. Too many shiny textures can cancel each other out; too many matt textures in an arrangement will look flat and boring.

It takes a while for an arranger to appreciate the subtleties of texture and the need not only for variety but also for repetition. It is not just in the plant material that it matters; one has to be equally aware of it with the container, base or accessory.

Space

The last, and least tangible, design element is space. It has always been a feature of Japanese flower arrangement (ikebana) but not of Western massed styles with their profusion of plant materials. In this century, however, space has come to be much more appreciated. Modern, freestyle designs use voids to balance solids and enclose spaces with looped stems, leaves or branches.

The Colour Wheel

Y   Yellow
YO   Yellow orange
O   Orange
RO   Red orange
R   Red
RV   Red violet
V   Violet
BV   Blue violet
B   Blue
BG   Blue green
G   Green
YG   Yellow green

Outer band
Pure hues

Band 2
*Tints (hues with
white added)*

Band 3
*Tones (hues with grey
added)*

Inner band
*Shades (hues with black
added)*

*There are many tints,
tones and shades of each
hue; only one of each is
shown.*

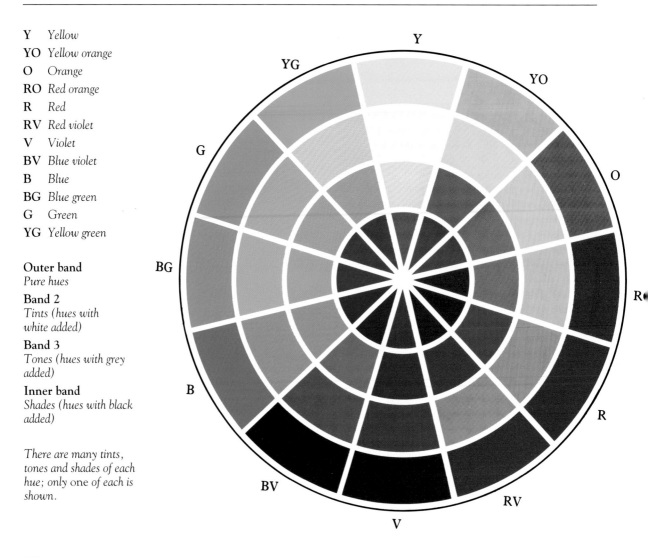

The Dimensions of Colour

Hue *refers to one colour
as distinct from another,
for example red as distinct
from green.*

Value *refers to the
lightness or darkness of a
colour, the modification
shown in tints, tones and
shades of a hue.*

Chroma *refers to the
amount of pure hue
present in a colour, the
strength or weakness of a
colour.*

*The term 'tone' is
generally used for any
colour deviating from a
pure colour.*

Neutrals, *or achromatic
colours, are black, white
and grey.*

*This diagram shows the
relationship between hue,
tint, tone, shade and
neutrals.*

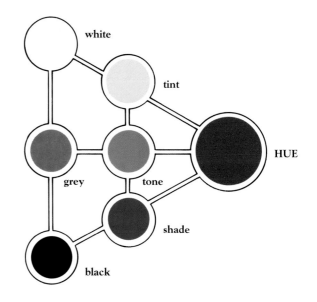

Basic Colour Schemes

Monochromatic
The use of tints, tones and shades of one colour

Analogous (Adjacent)
The use of two to four colours lying next to each other on the colour wheel

Complementary
The use of colours that lie opposite or approximately opposite each other on the colour circle

Triadic
The use of three colours equidistant apart

Polychromatic
The use of many colours together

These diagrams illustrate the principles of colour-scheme selection.

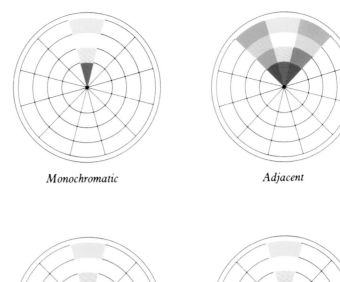

Monochromatic

Adjacent

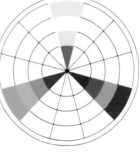

Complementary

Triadic

The flowers used in these pew-ends are in luminous colours and are therefore ideal in a dark church.

Vivid contrast is a feature of complementary colour schemes such as this, combining blue and orange.

JUST LEAVES

Learn to use leaves in an arrangement, not just as a foil to flowers but as features in their own right. They are much longer-lasting than cut flowers and have a quiet beauty. There is an enormous variety of sizes, shapes and textures and an astonishing range of greens, including many with white or yellow variegation. To these you can add the grey-leaved plants and the yellow, brown and darkish-red ones. Several that are easy to grow are used in the arrangement here, which has been inspired by the colours of the Spode plates in the 'Wild Flowers' series displayed on the grey-green wall behind.

OVERALL SIZE (W × H)
60 × 90 cm (24 × 36 in)

YOU WILL NEED

Tall container like this alabaster lamp base, fitted with a matching candlecup. Candlesticks, figurines and tall narrow-necked vases can be adapted this way.

MECHANICS

Cylinder or block of soaked floral foam

'Frog' and putty-type adhesive or sticky tape

PLANT MATERIAL

4 sprays eucalyptus

4 stems red berberis

Pine or cedar

Shrubby atriplex

3 leaves Mahonia bealei *or* M.x 'Charity'

Spray Rosa rubrifolia

2 sprays Pieris japonica 'Variegata'

Brown-tinged ivy

Plain green hosta leaves

2 sprays yellow privet (Ligustrum ovalifolium aureo-marginatum)

ARRANGER

Dorothy Kay

Even the tiniest garden or balcony can find room for a few useful cutting shrubs. Choose from the list on page 167. With some bought sprays from the florist, cuttings from a friend and one or two from the hedgerows, an inexpensive arrangement is possible at most times of the year.

1 · Make the candlecup secure in the base by using putty-type adhesive or tightening the screw if it has a screw fitting. Tape in the soaked foam and see that it protrudes at least 2.5 cm (1 in) above the candlecup rim. Ensure that there is space for watering. If the foam fits the cup well, cut a triangular wedge out of it at the back to allow the end of a long-spouted watering to be inserted. Candlecups do not hold much water and need to be topped up each day.

2 · Eucalyptus is used to make an asymmetrical outline of gently curving stems. The tallest is to the right of centre back, curving towards the left. It is roughly one-and-a-half times the height of the container to give good proportions. Two bulkier sprays extend from the left front and a balancing spray to the right.

3 · The red berberis, pine or cedar and shrubby atriplex follow the lines of the eucalyptus sprays in order to strengthen the outline. Three mahonia leaves fill in lower spaces in the outline and a spray of *Rosa rubrifolia* completes the framework to the left.

4 · A bushy piece of pieris takes a central position but slightly to the right. A cluster of ivy that has taken on an attractive tan colour (perhaps from soil deficiency or lack of watering) disguises the tape and provides a gentle colour link with the top plate, just as the dark red berberis picks up the pinky colour of the bottom one. The white variegation of the pieris justifies the choice of a creamy-white container.

5 · It remains now to give extra 'body' to the whole arrangement where the important features have already been established. Two or three hosta leaves are inserted low on the right and some higher on the left by the rose foliage. Because the tallest eucalyptus stem looks weak, a yellow privet spray is put in front and more yellow privet lower down on the left to repeat the yellow colouring. The foam is now quite honeycombed, so trim stems carefully.

Checking the Arrangement

● When cutting or buying leaves for arranging bear in mind that variation is needed in colour, shape, size and texture. It is possible to use all green leaves and still achieve variety in all these aspects, but there is no doubt that some variegation of yellow, cream or white attracts the eye and focuses attention in much the same way as colourful flowers do in a mixed arrangement. Use variegation as the dominant feature but use it with discretion or the whole effect can become muddled.

● A few larger, plain leaves (like the hostas here) are almost always needed, to provide visual weight and contrast to the smaller sprays.

● Above all, texture plays a very important part in making an effective group. If leaves are all shiny the result is monotonous, so some matt variations are needed such as ferns, cupressus, tellima, pelargonium, eucalyptus or hosta. Similarly, there should be enough different leaf shapes to give variety: the feathery types of pine, fern or cupressus; the ladder patterns of mahonia; the rosettes of pieris; and the plain rounds, triangles and diamonds of single leaves.

● In spring when the new growth starts, young leaves have very little body to help them hold water and they soon wilt when cut. If soaked in water for too long they become waterlogged and turn brown. With evergreen sprays it is often possible to nip out this very new growth and use the older parts of the stem. Otherwise it is best to boil the stem ends for 30 seconds (see page 14) and then give a deep drink. When leaves are very young even this may not work and the only answer is to wait until the plant has matured for a few more weeks.

Other Options

Any leaves and sprays can be used to make a foliage arrangement, as long as you have five varieties of leaf to give sufficient interest. The height might be made with strongly vertical leaves such as yucca, iris or phormium, but there will be a need also for curving, trailing sprays such as ivy, jasmine, rubus or tradescantia. Bushy fillers like holly, choisya, skimmia and hebe can be used and plain leaves such as arum, begonia, bergenia or tellima.

A Traditional Triangle

Western arrangers generally refer to a triangular-shaped mass arrangement as 'traditional' but it is very much a shape of the 20th century. The rather precise, narrow, pointed top was seldom seen before the 1950s, but since then it has become one of the most popular shapes, and indeed the hallmark, of British arrangers. It is at its most elegant as a pedestal arrangement with down-flowing trails (see pages 46–7), but here it is seen in a table-top version of bright mixed spring flowers.

OVERALL SIZE (W × H)

70 × 60 cm (28 × 24 in)

YOU WILL NEED

Footed bowl – ceramic, metal or alabaster

Tin to line it and hold mechanics

MECHANICS

½ block of soaked floral foam

Green sticky tape

Putty-type adhesive

PLANT MATERIAL

Rhamnus

Ferns

Rubus tricolor

Ivy (Hedera helix 'Goldheart')

Arum and bergenia leaves

10 or more different daffodils and narcissi

3 blue iris

Bunch of mimosa

Laurustinus

Forsythia

2 pink hyacinths

3 red/white parrot tulips, 3 other tulips

Mauve freesia

Hellebores

ARRANGER

Susan Phillips

1 · Condition spring flowers well. Those from the florist have often been forced and need time to take up plenty of water. The ferns, laurustinus, rhamnus, bergenia and ivy can stand in a bucket of water, but the arum leaves should be completely submerged in water for at least two hours.

2 · A suitably sized tin as a liner will help to protect a precious container from water marking. In this arrangement an alabaster tazza has been used and, as alabaster is not waterproof, the liner is essential.

3 · Place the block of soaked floral foam in the dish with a corner pointing towards the front. With the opposite corner at the back this gives maximum depth for the front and back stems, to avoid a flat look. Strap in the floral foam with crossed bands of sticky tape.

4 · The first stem is the variegated rhamnus as the central 'backbone' of the design; it goes well to the back of the foam. Use ferns and rubus to establish the width on the left and ferns and ivy on the right. The longest side stems will be about two-thirds the length of the backbone. The finished arrangement will be symmetrical,

ie balanced about the centre stem, but will gain interest from not having exact repetition on each side.

5 · A narcissus and an iris are placed behind and in front of the backbone stem, strengthening it and at the same time beginning to create a feeling of depth. Other flowers and leaves, such as the forsythia, narcissi and hellebores, put into the foam at an angle of about 45°, start to make the linking outline between the top and the sides.

6 · The bergenia leaves (back left) and arum leaves (forward and right) cover some of the foam and lower stems and make a setting for the central pink hyacinths, the largest mass of all the flowers, which will be added next.

7 · The lovely parrot tulips, coming well forward over the container rim, carry the pink right through the arrangement from the tulip at the top right.

8 · The yellow, cream and white colourings are echoed all around the design by adding daffodils, mimosa and laurustinus. The mauve freesia on the left, while not exactly the same colour as the two irises, is sufficiently toning to balance them. In turn, the purple markings on the fine hellebores pick up the freesia colour and bring a rhythmic line across the pink one.

Checking the Arrangement

● One of the traps that beginners often fall into is that of cutting too short the stems for the centre front of the arrangement. This immediately gives an undercut, punched-in look and often leaves visible the hard line of the edge of the container. Err on the side of having these important front flowers too long – it is quite easy to shorten them as the arrangement takes shape.

● Another fault often met with in early days of arranging is that of having the backbone stem leaning slightly forward. Subsequent stems tend to follow suit and the result is a forward-tilting, perhaps even over-balancing, arrangement.

● A similar problem occurs if the backbone stem is put in too near the front of the foam, leaving insufficient room for later stems, so that the front becomes crowded and crumpled.

Other Options

Other options are limited only by what is available. This shaped arrangement can be done at any season, using preserved or fresh plant materials. Alternatives to the arrangement shown here include one done exclusively in foliage; one in tints, tones and shades of a single colour; and one in brilliant primaries. It can be several centimetres (a couple of inches) high or from floor to ceiling, on a pedestal or in a low bowl. The choice is yours.

A LOW CENTREPIECE

The first thing most newcomers want to do when they come to a course of lessons is a centrepiece for a luncheon or dinner table. It is usually for a slightly more formal occasion, such as a wedding anniversary, Christmas dinner or a special birthday. The colourful arrangement in the picture, with candles included, could either be a central display or one of a pair at each end of a longer table. The colour link between flowers, candles, linen and china makes an impact as soon as guests take their seats at table.

OVERALL SIZE (W×D×H)
70×30×30 cm (28×12 ×12 in)

YOU WILL NEED
Shallow plastic oblong dish
3 candles 25 cm (10 in) high

MECHANICS
Oblong block of floral foam
Green sticky tape
Cocktail sticks/toothpicks

PLANT MATERIAL
Long, fine foliage like ivy, stephanandra, berberis (red and/or green), jasmine
Bushier sprigs: privet, box, heather
Single leaves: tellima, heuchera, ivy
Flowers: 10 roses, 6–8 stems dendrobium orchids, sprays of tea-tree flower (Leptospermum), small cluster flowers or spray carnations

ARRANGER
Christine Buckey

1 · First cut the foam block if necessary so that it fits the dish with a little space all around for watering. It should protrude above the dish by about 4 cm (1½ in). Soak the block in water *for a few minutes only* until it sinks below the surface of the water in a bowl or bucket or in the sink. Don't leave it to soak too long or the foam will break up more easily when stems are inserted. Strap the foam into the dish, taking the tape right over the dish to overlap the tape ends underneath.

2 · Prepare the candles by securely taping four cocktail sticks evenly spaced around the bottom of each candle and protruding by two-thirds of their length. These will hold the candles in the foam but they will not make large holes, nor take up space needed for flower and leaf stems. Adjust the heights so that the tops are not quite level, to give a gentler line.

3 · Establish the overall length and width of the arrangement with long, fine leaf sprays or orchids. Beware of bringing plant material of any kind too high at the base of the candles. The candles should stand well

clear so that they can be lit and burn safely during the meal. Never leave them burning unattended.

4 · Now work towards the centre using shorter stems and bushier pieces to start covering the foam and making a background for the larger flowers. Use the single, larger leaves near the base of the candles and to complete masking the foam. Remember that this arrangement will be seen from close to, and guests will not enjoy looking at the mechanics.

5 · Finally add the roses and orchids. Cut some orchid stems carefully in two, to give a short stem of buds and one of more open flowers to use nearer the centre for good visual balance and a focus of interest.

Checking the Arrangement

● Take the inspiration for the colours of candles and flowers from the linen or china that is to be used, or from the occasion if it is a special one, such as Easter, Christmas, Hallowe'en or a wedding anniversary. If colours are co-ordinated the impact is far greater. Here the bright pink of the flowers on the Royal Albert 'Village Green' service is echoed in the placemats and napkins on the mahogany table. Tints, tones and shades of the colour are picked up again in the candles and flowers. Varying tones give more interest to a flower arrangement than exact colour matching does. The various

greens in the dinner service are picked up by the greens of the leaves.
● When a table is set for dining, whether formally or less so, it is best to concentrate on the colour scheme of the table itself, without trying to co-ordinate it with other colours in the room décor generally. As Constance Spry wrote: 'It is the table that will be the cynosure of all eyes.'

Other Options

Different colour schemes to try will depend on china and table linen. Don't be afraid to take a sample of linen or china with you when you go to buy flowers. Candles and paper napkins can often be purchased in matching sets to ring the changes for informal meals.

A Silver Wedding celebration could have silvery pussy willow with cream or white narcissi, anemones or roses. A yellow colour scheme is lovely in spring with forsythia, mimosa and daffodils. In autumn there are berried branches to use with pom-pom dahlias in the orange colour range, or Michaelmas daisies with spray carnations or chrysanthe-mums to pick up pinks, mauves and blues.

BUFFET PARTY FLOWERS

Buffet party flowers need to be striking and raised from the table, as guests will be seeing them from a standing, rather than a seated, position. As with a sitting-down meal, the style and colour scheme for the flowers can take their cue from the china and linen, from the occasion or, in this case, from the room décor since the focus of attention is less on the table itself and more on the room generally.

OVERALL SIZE (W × H)
75 × 90 cm (30 × 36 in)

YOU WILL NEED
*Two-tier metal stand in black
(available from floral accessory
suppliers and some garden centres
and florists' shops)
2 yellow candles 30 cm (12 in)
high
2 lime-green circular bases,
20 cm (8 in) and 25 cm (10 in)
in diameter
Tin or block to go between bases*

MECHANICS
*2 rounds soaked floral foam
Green sticky tape
Cocktail sticks/toothpicks*

PLANT MATERIAL
*12 leaves spider plant
6 sprays spotted laurel (aucuba)
10 seedheads (green) of grape
hyacinth
10 yellow iris
3 orange and 2 yellow lilies
6 each lemons and peaches
Bunch of green grapes*

ARRANGER
Wendy Barrett

1 · Place the largest base in position, put the tin or block on top of it and place the smaller base on top of that. Use the tape to secure a round of soaked foam in each dish of the stand. Put the stand on the top base.

2 · Tape four cocktail sticks, evenly spaced, to the bottom of each candle, with two-thirds of each stick extending beyond the candle end. Place the candles at slightly uneven heights towards the back of the top round of foam.

3 · Begin at the top with the spider plant leaves. Insert them on the right into the *side* of the foam, not the top, to follow the curve of the stand. Put sprays and individual leaves of spotted laurel into each container . Add the grape hyacinth seedheads, which have been chosen for their shape and texture.

4 · The yellow iris stems come next; the heads should follow the spider plant curve in the top container and reach up towards it from the bottom one. The orange lilies are clustered on the left at the top, with one or two single flowers cut off to use in the bottom dish.

5 · Now add the fruit, using cocktail sticks (two to each fruit if needed) to anchor them into the foam or into each other.

6 · The yellow lilies are used as a final focal point, and the foam should be well covered by now. Cut one lemon in half to introduce a new pattern and texture. Place on the cloth with the remaining fruit.

Checking the Arrangement

● The orange drink and glasses and the yellow cloth and napkins complete a fresh and tangy colour scheme, which was deliberately chosen with the bright greeny-blue wall in mind. The serving dishes were set out to the left on the long sideboard.
● It is very important that raised flowers should be very stable and the mechanics well secured, as there will be a lot of movement on and around the serving table.
● The stand used here is metal

and has an elegant curve supporting the top container, but it is possible to contrive a rather similar home-made version. A curving piece of driftwood, or stripped ivy, can be screwed to a wooden base, with a screw-in candlecup at the top. Or use a dowel rod for the upright (though it lacks a curve), with a small flower-pot saucer screwed to the top. Paint either version or leave the driftwood natural.

Other Options

This comparatively simple design can be repeated in all seasons of the year. The fruit can easily be adapted to the season and the colours needed.

The curves of the spider plant and the accenting yellow iris are the important rhythmic lines to find substitutes for. In spring this might be done with new-budding branches, or pussy willow, again with irises. In summer there are blossoming shrubs, jasmine, honeysuckle and ivy. Autumn berries are usually in curved sprays and these go well with apples, pears and dahlias. At Christmas holly or ivy will provide down-curving sprays to use with evergreens and fruit. Or, if you want to prepare well in advance, it can be done with artificial flowers and gold and silver plastic leaves.

STILL LIFE GROUP

The flower arranger is constantly learning about shapes, forms and textures and how to compose them into pleasing groups. There is no better exercise than trying to make a still life group of fruit and vegetables without any flowers. Painters of still life delight in portraying different textures, the roundness of jugs, the highlights on glass and metal and the variations of shape in fruits and flowers. The arranger can find equal pleasure in assembling the real things.

OVERALL SIZE (W×D×H)
75×30×38 cm (30×12 ×15 in)

YOU WILL NEED
Pitcher about 38 cm (15 in) high
Dish, small bowl, mug
Terracotta pots, boxes or tins to create different levels

PLANT MATERIAL
Vegetable marrow (yellow)
6 squashes of different sizes and colour
4 small squashes
Bunch of beetroot with leaves
7 shallots
5 small turnips
6 sprays bramble with berries
Green moss
5 apples
Kent cobs (filberts) and walnuts

ARRANGER
Gloria Nicol

1 · None of the items needs to be in water, except the bramble stems in the mug. The beetroot leaves should be submerged in water for an hour or so.

2 · Set the pitcher at the back, about one-third along from the right, with the marrow standing upright next to it.

3 · Group the squashes to the left and right, raising them on pots if necessary as can be seen on the right of the picture. Note how the different colours are used to balance each other. There is an orange squash showing importantly on the right and another tucked down on the left. The yellow one in the extreme right picks up the yellow of the marrow. The two white ones, which are large and would be eye-catching, are partially obscured by later placements.

4 · Lay the bundle of beetroot diagonally on the left, propped up as needed on a pot. The stems are important in providing diagonal lines to contrast with the mainly rounded forms, and echo the line of the tilted squash at top right. Arrange the shallots in the bowl and the berried bramble in a mug of water (to ensure the leaves don't flop) and position them as in the picture. Set an attractive dish to the right front and fill with baby squashes and/or berries.

5 · Now tuck fresh moss around the front of the groups already in place. Group the turnips centrally by the dish, the apples to the left (with two on the right) and the nuts left of centre. Add more moss if needed and mist-spray the beetroot leaves.

Checking the Arrangement

● The success of such a group lies in the repetition and contrast of forms, colours and textures. Many fruits and vegetables are round, or nearly so, but some are shiny and others matt. Take advantage of this and put the two sorts next to each other. Repeat the round shapes but vary the sizes. Here the squashes are round and shiny, the beetroot are round and matt, the apples are in-between, the walnuts differently textured and

the blackberries round but tiny. The glazed jug echoes this roundness in the shape of its body and the curve of the handle; so do the plate, the bowl, the mug and even the terracotta pot on which the large orange gourd is set. The contrast comes in the beetroot and bramble leaves, the stalks and rough-textured moss.

● The still-life groups we see in paintings tend to use rather more objects than fruit, flowers and vegetables. Many of them are household items, pottery or kitchen utensils. Very often fabric is introduced as a tablecloth or nearby curtain. The flower arranger probably uses less because competitive work at shows calls for the plant material to predominate. At home, however, one can forget this requirement and indulge in setting up a little group just because the colour catches one's eye. Have you noticed here, for example, how the purple-pink colour is picked up in the beetroot, turnips, apples and unripe blackberries?

Other Options

This sort of still-life group can be used in the kitchen or outside for a barbecue decoration. Indoors, on a sideboard, table centre or shelf, fruit and foliage probably make a more appropriate display. Flowers can certainly be added if you wish. There are no rules.

In the home it helps to assemble the still life on a base, tray, piece of basketry, pastry board or fabric-covered cake drum, or even on a bunched piece of fabric.

Chapter two · Review

lower arranging is often called 'floral art', which emphasizes that it is as much concerned with art and design as it is with flowers, berries, leaves and fruits. Artists in any medium, including flower arrangers, work with the so-called design elements. These are the physical qualities of colour, form/shape, line, texture and space. Once understood, they can be consciously used to design and to improve arrangements.

Colour

This is the quality that makes the most immediate, and often the most lasting, impression. We identify and remember 'the house with the blue front door'.

Colour can be used to highlight an occasion: yellow for Golden Wedding anniversary flowers, pink for a baby girl's christening or orange and black for Hallowe'en, for example.

Colour can create a mood: yellow for sunshine and happiness, green for coolness, grey and mauve for grief and clashing reds for excitement. In fact, it is colour most of all that is responsible for the emotional impact of a flower arrangement.

INFLUENCES ON COLOUR

Colour is affected by different types of lighting:
Daylight gives the truest colour values.
Electric tungsten (ordinary household lighting) enhances red, orange and yellow and tends to deaden blue and purple.
Fluorescent lighting makes blue and purple vibrant, muddies red to brown and neutralizes yellow.
Candlelight has the same effect as tungsten but, as it is dimmer, blue, purple and all dark colours generally appear black.

In poor light use luminous colours – white, cream, yellow, yellow-green, orange and the paler tints of other colours.

Colour is also affected by texture. A shiny surface brightens a colour; a matt finish darkens it.

VARIATIONS IN COLOUR SCHEMES

Polychromatic means many colours used together, as in the picture on page 111. *Monochromatic* means tints, tones and shades of one hue. Within each main hue there are many variations, from the palest tint (with lots of white in it) to the darkest shade (with black in it) and greyed tones. *Complementary* refers to colours opposite each other on the colour wheel. *Analogous* means up to four colours adjacent to each other on it. *Triadic* involves three colours equal distances apart on the wheel.

On page 33 the leaf colours vary from almost white to a green that is almost black, with some veering towards yellow and others towards blue or brown. The human eye can detect many variations in colour. Practise looking at a colour and trying to analyse whether it is a yellowish-green or a blue-tinged green, whether a pink has a lot of yellow in it (peach) or a lot of blue (heather). Subtle colour changes in an arrangement can add interest.

Form and Shape

Leaf shapes are very varied. They may be circular, triangular, oval or blade-like, ranging in size from tiny leaflets to huge fan-shaped palms.

Flowers may be daisy-like with a mounded centre and many ray-like petals (for example, gerbera). They may be cup-petalled (for instance, a rose), bell-shaped (a lily) or shaped like a spike (a gladiolus).

Fruits and vegetables are often rounded, but may be oval and triangular.

Line

This is simply a long, narrow version of form. The line of a stem, curving branch, twisting vine or blade-shaped leaf often establishes the height and outline of an arrangement and gives rhythm to the design. (More about rhythm in Chapter 3).

Texture

This is the surface quality of an object: how it *feels* and how it *looks*. In flower arrangement visual texture is more important than tactile texture. An unglazed pot will look rough, a leaf shiny, a stem hairy.

Each picture shows many variations in texture. Count up the different textures, and the shapes, of the leaves on page 33. On pages 40–1 is a study of three-dimensional forms and textures. Smooth shiny squashes contrast with matt beetroot and its leaves, walnuts and moss.

Space

Space is not always easy to visualize as a positive quality in design, but it is important in most flower arrangements. It enables individual flowers and leaves to be seen and enjoyed and it frames the whole arrangement. Most flowers actually contain some space within themselves: in the cup-shape of roses, the bell-shape of campanulas and in the gaps between the florets of blossom on a branch, for example.

The space in which an arrangement is to be placed will affect its size and outline and whether it is tall and narrow or low but wide.

Depth, the third spatial dimension, is created in an arrangement by using flowers and leaves at the back, to avoid a 'cardboard cut-out' look. To the beginner it may seem to be a waste of flowers and leaves because they are hardly seen, but the difference they make is surprising.

Equipment You Have Acquired

CONTAINERS

Bowl, footed or on a short plinth

Low dish

Shallow plastic oblong dish

Trough

2 painted tins/small unobtrusive dishes

Tall lamp-base or candlestick fitted with a candlecup

Metal stand with high and low containers

MECHANICS

Pinholder

Wire mesh with 5 cm (2 in) holes

Green floral foam

Plastic 'frogs'

Putty-type adhesive

Stub, rose and reel wires

Candleholders

Pack of cocktail sticks/toothpicks

ACCESSORIES

Model bird, nest and eggs

Candles in Christmas and party colours

BASES

Round or oval base covered with hessian/burlap

Chapter Three

A LITTLE MORE DIFFICULT

Whereas the design elements are the physical qualities of plant material and what we look at when we choose them for arranging, how we put them together is governed by another set of factors: the principles of design. The seven principles are balance, proportion, scale, rhythm, contrast, dominance and harmony. None of these principles is difficult to apply, but in the excitement of arranging and enjoying the flowers, one may get overlooked. If, perhaps, there is not enough contrast in colour, in shape or in texture, or if the visual balance is not quite right, try to correct it straightaway.

*T*o ensure *that* you don't miss out any of the principles, check back through each in turn. (A mnemonic for remembering them, found useful by students over the years, is Big Pink Stones Roll Constantly Down Hill.) After you become experienced in flower arranging, you'll find that taking the principles into account becomes second nature and you do so automatically.

Balance

It is visual balance that is important to flower arrangers; lack of visual stability makes us all feel uncomfortable. An arrangement must not look lopsided, top-heavy or as though it is leaning backwards or forwards. (Good, well-secured mechanics can often correct and sustain physical imbalance, but we have all known arrangements that actually do fall over; it happens in almost every show, even at the National Competitions!)

The balance may be symmetrical, with even sizes and 'weight' on either side of a central vertical or backbone (see page 47), or asymmetrical, where heavier, larger forms on one side may balance longer, narrower lines on the other or an upward curve to the right is balanced by a downward curve on the left (see page 49). The landscape on page25 is a good example of asymmetric balance. The heavy bottom-right grouping counteracts the top branches leading the eye away to the left, and the conifer and snowdrops act as a full stop to this.

Proportion and Scale

These are not quite the same thing, but most people use the terms interchangeably. Scale is a size relationship of one thing to another, and proportion relates more to quantities, distances and areas.

One cannot do better than quote from Jean Taylor's *Creative Flower Arrangement*: 'In a flower arrangement, each flower in relation to the container is scale, but the amount of plant material in relation to the container is proportion.'

The golden section is a mathematical statement of the ideal proportions when a line or area is divided in two. In it the whole is to the larger part as that part is to the smaller part. These parts are approximately equal to two-thirds and one-third – proportions that are used by flower arrangers as a rough guide to the ideal lengths of stems in relation to the container or base, and the ideal width of an arrangement in relation to its height.

Scale and proportion are important in all arrangements but especially so in miniature designs, in which a component that is out of scale sticks out like a sore thumb. Similarly, in landscape scenes (page 25) and the petite arrangement (page 51), one item which is out of scale can destroy the whole illusion of a Lilliputian world.

Rhythm

Rhythm is a sense of movement or 'flow' giving life and cohesion to any design and certainly to flower arrangements. Rhythm can be created by line plant material (stems, branches); repetition of shapes, colours and textures; radiation (fanning out from a single container); or the grading of sizes and shapes (from buds to fully open flowers) and of pale tints to dark shades of one colour.

Contrast

While rhythm is being created by flowing lines, repetition, radiation and gradation, there is also a need for contrast, with opposites. This contrast can be slight, when it is usually called variation; or it may be extreme – from straight lines to solid spheres (for example, the candles and round flowers opposite and on pages 21 and 37) or from one complementary colour to the other (such as orange and blue on page 53). Quite often the setting for an arrangement may provide the contrast of colour.

Dominance

Dominance is sometimes called emphasis. A focusing feature is needed in most arrangements, and this may be achieved with something of larger size, brighter colour or shinier texture.

In traditional, massed arrangements this dominant feature (often called a focal point or area) is likely to be central and near the rim of the container and the point from which the stems radiate. In freestyle, abstract and parallel designs, dominant features may be in various places; these eye-catching features will then affect the overall balance and will need to be compensated for.

In competitive work (see Chapter 8) the plant material must always predominate over all other components. Background, bases and accessories should never catch the eye first and must always play a subordinate role.

Harmony

Harmony or unity is achieved when all parts of a design fit together and there is no jarring feature. In a flower arrangement it is achieved by the careful and creative use of well-chosen plant materials put together with due regard to all the design principles that are discussed here.

A FLOOR PEDESTAL

The graceful, flowing pedestal arrangement is often thought to be the pièce de résistance of British arranging and yet it is really no more difficult than an arrangement on a table. It is just larger and needs longer stems and some bigger flowers and leaves. It looks splendid in foliage alone, but here it is a typical combination of flowers and leaves from garden and florist and makes use of fresh new foliage in spring.

OVERALL SIZE (W×H)
90 × 185 cm (36 × 72 in)

YOU WILL NEED
Column or wrought-iron stand about 108 cm (42 in) high
Plastic or ceramic bowl 23 cm (9 in) in diameter and about 8 cm (3 in) deep

MECHANICS
1½ large blocks of soaked floral foam
Green sticky tape and putty-type adhesive
Piece of 2.5 cm (1 in) wire mesh to cover foam if very thick stems are being used

PLANT MATERIAL
4 leaves globe artichoke or cardoon (Cynara scolymus)
3 leaves Fatsia japonica
1–2 sprays of hebe foliage or similar small-leaved shrubs
3 stems Euphorbia wulfenii
7 sprays flowering currant (ribes)
5–7 stems snowball tree (Viburnum opulus 'Sterile')
5 stems pink larkspur (Delphinium consolida)
5 deep pink roses (these are 'Jacaranda')
10 ranunculus
5 cream lilies

ARRANGER
Avril Hill

1 · Into the container place a block of soaked foam at the back and a half block in front. Fix securely with tapes crossed at right angles and taken right over the foam and under the bowl. For stability, wire or tape the bowl to the column or pedestal stand. Trouble taken over securing the mechanics is never wasted.

2 · Make an outline with three stems of the snowball tree (or similar). The tallest is placed well back in the large block of foam and should be at least as long as the pedestal or column and up to one-and-a-half times as tall. The curving side stems go into the *sides* of the lower block of foam. They should be almost (at least two-thirds) the length of the tallest stem.

3 · The outer points of the framework established, strengthen them with two tall stems of larkspur in the centre, the remaining snowball branches, three cardoon or artichoke leaves on the left and one at the back and two fatsia leaves at the right. Fill in at the back with hebe foliage to provide a contrast of size and shape. Bring a spray forward to help cover the foam and tape.

4 · The stems of pink flowering currant are next, placed to follow the original outline sprays and with heavier sprays downwards on the right.

5 · Add two heads of euphorbia at top left and a third centrally to the right. A line of deep pink roses and a stem of larkspur on the left help to balance the currant sprays on the other side. Use the ranunculus to fill in gaps where colour is needed. The cream lilies provide the rich, bulky finishing touch.

6 · Fill the container with water. If possible, treat the arrangement to a fine misting spray of water to help reduce transpiration. A large group of flowers and leaves like this takes up and then gives off a lot of water especially in the first 24 hours.

Checking the Arrangement

● However dissimilar the two sides of the arrangement are, they must look balanced. This applies to colour, length of stems and the size and density of the flowers and leaves used.

● Take care that the finished pedestal does not look top-heavy. Here the solid-looking black column prevents that.

Other Options

For the beginner tackling this large type of arrangement it is safer to use flowers within one colour range. With more experience it is exciting to try, say, clashing reds or trickier yellows, blues and purples.

The black marbled column used here is in fact home-made from large conduit piping and is perhaps a little dark and weighty for the arrangement. A wrought-iron pedestal could have been used instead. Stands can be bought that are adjustable from about 60 cm (24 in) to 110 cm (43 in). Some pedestals have integral containers but, if not, a plastic bulb bowl or a cake tin will be suitable if painted to match the stand. It will not show when the arrangement is complete.

USING A BOX

A lidded box can make an attractive container for flowers. It is also an economical choice because the open lid provides a backing for the arrangement and fewer flowers and leaves are therefore needed. An old writing box, tea caddy, workbox or cutlery canteen can be used, as long as it has a hinged lid that can be propped open. Use a stick from the hedgerow as a prop – it will be less noticeable and largely hidden by the finished arrangement.

OVERALL SIZE (W × H)
50 × 50 cm (20 × 20 in)

YOU WILL NEED
Lidded box about 30 × 20 cm (12 × 8 in)

Casserole dish or plastic box to hold water and stand inside the first box

MECHANICS
Piece of soaked floral foam

Green sticky tape or pronged foam holder

PLANT MATERIAL
Flowering branches or small-leaved sprays of foliage

Round leaves or bushy sprays, such as ivy, bergenia, arum, tellima

Mixture of garden/florist's flowers with variations in shape and size (include some buds) in tints, tones and shades of one main colour (pink is used here)

ARRANGER
Anne Blunt

---

1 · Fix the piece of soaked foam in the inner container using tape or a foam holder. The foam should come 2.5 cm (1 in) above the rim of the liner *and* the outer box. If the outer box is very deep, raise the liner on a small block of wood or a flower-pot saucer to get the

level right. While arranging, take care not to hide all the lid. The finished arrangement should show almost half the lid or there will be no point in having chosen the box in the first place.

2 · Place the outline flowers or foliage in a sweeping S-curve to give an interesting asymmetry to the arrangement, high on one side and low on the other. Add shorter stems to strengthen the first placements and to give an outline for the other two corners.

3 · Use larger leaves to cover the foam, bringing one or two forward over the box rim. This is why it is useful to have the foam above the edge of the box because these stems are put into the side of the foam. The bolder forms' help to focus interest at the centre of the arrangement and relieve the fussiness of the smaller leaves.

4 · Follow the established outline of the arrangement with small flowers (for example, spray carnations, broom or other flowers in bud).

5 · Save the largest flowers (open roses, carnations, phlox) to use towards the centre of the box. The focus of interest – which is where, for good balance, these larger flowers should be – is more or less at the point where the longest upright stem goes into the floral foam.

6 · Because the lid is only partly open it is very important that the arrangement should not look squashed, but just comfortably backed and protected by the lid. On the other hand, if only a few flowers are available, close the lid a little by shortening the stick propping it open.

Checking the Arrangement

● The lazy 'S' line used here is often known as a 'Hogarth curve' because the painter, William Hogarth, once called this line made of reversed curves 'the line of beauty'. Although very loose, the line should be discernible.
● The flowers coming forward over the front rim, as well as the leaves, help to give depth to the design.
● If the inside lid of the box is unattractive, or perhaps has lettering on it, a lining can be simply made by cutting a piece of

cardboard just smaller than the inside lid measurements and covering it with plain velvet, satin, dupion or matt brushed nylon. Glue the fabric to the *back* of the card only. Tuck this into the lid, unglued side out, and it will be held firmly enough. It is good to have several lid liners in various colours to set off different-coloured arrangements. On the other hand, a soft grey-green will suit almost anything.

Other Options

Almost any flowers, leaves and berries from any season are suitable for this type of arrangement, provided they are not too large for the size of the box. Smaller boxes, even down to a tiny trinket box, can also be used, with miniature flowers and leaves, perhaps garnered from rockery plants. More about small arrangements on pages 50–1.

SMALL BUT PERFECT

Tiny things are always appealing and the miniature class at a flower arrangement show is a great attraction to visitors. For competitive work a miniature has usually to be less than 10 cm (4 in) in length, width and height. Petite is less than 23 cm (9 in) and generally larger than a miniature. Pictured here are a freestyle miniature in dried plant material and a petite landscape using dried and fresh material.

OVERALL SIZE (W × D × H)

Petite: *within a cube 23 × 23 × 23 cm (9 × 9 × 9 in)*

Miniature: *within a cube 10 × 10 × 10 cm (4 × 4 × 4 in)*

YOU WILL NEED

Petite: *Circular base 15 cm (6 in) covered with matt green fabric*

Miniature: *Tiny ceramic pot, 2 cardboard bases each 6 cm × 5cm (2½ in × 1 in), balsa wood square plinth*

For both arrangements: *Nail scissors, cocktail sticks (for making holes in foam), clear instant adhesive, water-colour paints, matt spray fixative*

MECHANICS

Petite: *Piece of soaked floral foam, cling film*

Miniature: *Piece of dry (brown) foam*

PLANT MATERIAL

Petite: *Apple tree branch, dried guelder rose florets, green moss, yellow lichen, tiny cyclamen leaves, heuchera leaves, tips of ferns, yellow hypericum flowers, 1 or 2 berries, dried daisies*

Miniature: *Twist of clematis vine, dried cyclamen leaves, dried leaves of Hebe pageii, curls from a protea flower, cyclamen seedheads, 3 celastrus berries (dried to open out)*

ARRANGER

Ilona Barney

The Petite

Less demanding, in many ways, than a miniature arrangement, the petite also has a wider range of possible uses. It is an ideal size for bedside table flowers, for a dressing table or writing desk, or as a gift for a hostess or someone in hospital. Because the mechanics are not so fiddly, watering is much easier as it is more get-at-able. There are far more flowers and leaves of the right size.

1 · The base shown here is a 15 cm (6 in) circle of fabric-covered cardboard painted with water-colour and fixed with spray. The paint could be applied directly to the cardboard, using either water-colour paint and a brush, or car spray paint.

2 · The piece of apple wood was cut and reconstructed to make a pleasing 'tree' that would stand up on its own. The left-hand curved piece is also free-standing. Place it towards the back of the base with the right-hand curve coming farthest forward. Glue on the tiny dried flowers. Wedge a small piece of soaked foam, with the bottom wrapped in cling film to prevent dripping, at the base of the tree. Put green moss at the base of the tree and the right-hand curve and a little piece of yellow lichen in the centre.

3 · Insert into the foam the leaves, fern tips (so that they come well forward at the back) and the stems of the berries. Keep the forward placements on each side curving towards each other, but leaving the centre open.

4 · Insert the little hypericum flowers into the foam. Put the dried daisies into the moss on the right. The yellow berries and cyclamen leaves that are on the left in the first photograph were later replaced by ferns in the completed arrangement for better visual balance.

The Miniature

1 · It helps (especially to keep to size for competitive shows) to work on two pieces of cardboard 10 × 10 cm (4 × 4 in) glued at right-angles to represent a cube. Paint the two bases (one slightly smaller than the other) and balsa wood plinth with watercolour and, when they are dry, fix with matt spray fixative (available from artist's suppliers). Watercolour paint was used in order to get the exact colour that would tone with the pot.

2 · Glue the tiny piece of dry foam to the pot. Stand the pot on the plinth about one-third along the bases, which are staggered.

3 · Bend the clematis curl into a pleasing shape (softening it in steam from a boiling kettle if necessary) and insert one end into the foam, allowing the other end to curve across the front of the foam.

4 · Arrange the dried cyclamen leaves behind and in front of the clematis stem and a cluster of hebe leaves to the back left. The protea curls are also placed at the back left and the cyclamen seedheads diagonally at the right front.

5 · The celastrus berries form the focus of interest. To complete the asymmetrical balance, one berry is glued to a nest of leaves on the base.

Checking the Arrangement

● With these small arrangements the most important thing is the scale of each of the components in relation to the rest. One flower or leaf that is too large destroys the whole illusion and strikes a jarring note. If the picture of each arrangement could be blown up to full-page size, without the pen, scissors, or cocktail stick to act as a measure, it should not be possible to say whether the original was 10 cm (4 in) or 40 cm (16 in).

● Using fresh plant material in a miniature design does require patience and deft fingers, but this comes with practice. One develops a keen eye for spotting tiny florets, leaves and seedheads that will add interest to such small arrangements.
● In competitive shows more exhibits are disqualified or penalized for being over-size in the miniature and petite classes than in all the rest put together. Work well within the size allowed. For miniatures, work to 9 cm (3½ in) rather than 10 cm (4 in) to be safe; for petites, work to 20 cm (8 in) instead of 23 cm (9 in) for the same reason.

Other Options

Any style is possible as a miniature or petite, and at any time of the year. Plant materials can be fresh or dried. This last is the easiest of all as there is no need for a water supply and many things can be glued in place. For fresh materials go into the garden, countryside or flower shop and 'think tiny'. Imagine a miniaturized version of the vertical design on page 19 and the New Zealand flax leaves become the tips of carnation leaves; the hosta leaves are variegated box and the flowers are hawthorn blossom. It's just a question of scale.

BRILLIANT CONTRAST

Traditional British arranging tends to favour colour schemes that are monochromatic or analogous, ranging through tints, tones and shades of one colour (eg pink through rose to dark red) or are closely grouped (eg cream, yellow, apricot, orange and brown). Contrasting or complementary pairs of colours, which lie opposite each other on a colour wheel, can be combined to create a sharper and bolder impact. Blue and orange (the other pairs are red/green and yellow/purple) are combined here in brilliant contrast.

different angles to give depth to the arrangement and to create different outlines. The mass of orange colour is grouped centrally.

OVERALL SIZE (W ×H)
70 × 80 cm (27 × 32 in)

YOU WILL NEED
A square or round black container 25–30 cm (10–12 in) across

MECHANICS
*Block of soaked floral foam
Large 'frog'*

PLANT MATERIAL
*2 blue delphiniums
9 orange gerberas
9 pale blue agapanthus
2 orange lilies
Chunky piece of driftwood painted matt black (optional)
2 clipped palm fans painted/ sprayed gloss black*

ARRANGER
Michael Bowyer

1 · Make sure that the soaked foam is firmly anchored on the 'frog' and that it protrudes well above the rim of the container. It will be holding 24 thick stems with heavy heads, so it needs to be thoroughly secure.

2 · Insert the delphiniums, one shorter than the other by some 10 cm (4 in), towards the back of

the foam. All of the foliage is removed so that the softness of green leaves does not reduce the colour impact.

3 · Lay the driftwood over the container at the front right-hand corner and insert the palm fans at the back left. The wood is optional, but it does create an interesting contrast to the shiny geometric shapes of the container and the palm fans, and provides an effective visual counter-balance to the fans.

4 · Now add the gerberas, more or less in a double, but uneven, line, bringing the lowest one well forward on a long stem. Try to turn the faces of the flowers at

5 · The agapanthus form a strong diagonal line of blue brought through from the back right corner to the front left.

6 · Two orange lilies at front right give a change of shape from the gerberas, yet echo the small trumpet shapes of the agapanthus florets and so have a design link.

Checking the Arrangement

● The arrangement is photographed against an abstract pattern created by spraying red, grey and deep blue on to a yellow 1.5 cm (½ in) chipboard base. It highlights the complementary colours by repeating them in a different combination and medium.
● Green is kept to a minimum, showing only in the stems, as it cools down the other colours.
● Red, orange and yellow are regarded as 'advancing' and 'warmer' colours because they seem nearer and look hotter to the viewer than the 'receding' and 'cooler' green, blue and purple. With a complementary colour scheme one is using an advancing colour with a receding one and

this means that a greater quantity or area of the receding colour is needed. In the picture there are far more blue than orange flowers.
● In arranging complementary colours, each colour need not be used at its full value, in other words the full brightness of the hue. An equally attractive combination can be achieved with dark navy blue and pale apricot. Red and green can be combined as pink (a pale tint of red) and pine (one of the darkest shades of green), or eau-de-nil (pale green tint) with burgundy (a deep red shade). The yellow/ purple complementaries are the most difficult to arrange together because yellow is so luminous and advancing and purple in its darker shades is the least luminous and almost black. However, the tints of yellow – say, cream or lemon – with tints of purple, ie lilac, group very successfully.

Other Options

In spring bright yellow forsythia and tulips could be arranged with purple iris and anemones. In autumn, mauve and purple michaelmas daisies work well with the orange berries of cotoneaster or pyracantha and with orange dahlias. The blue spikes of aconitum are charming with lemon-yellow dahlias or black-eyed susans.

DOUBLE FEATURE

Two almost identical arrangements, close together, clearly show the rhythmic value of repeated parallel lines, colours and shapes. Raising one, and adding a small group at its base, makes what would have been boring repetition into an arresting double feature, using identical containers. Everything is arranged in strong vertical groups of each type of flower with colours grouped together to make bold statements.

OVERALL SIZE (W × H)
60 × 90 cm (24 × 36 in)

YOU WILL NEED
2 identical square terracotta pots 15 cm (6 in) high
Hessian-covered base 60 × 30 cm (24 × 12 in)
Small hessian-covered block 15 cm (6 in) square × 5 cm (2 in) high

MECHANICS
Soaked floral foam to fill each pot with about 4 cm (1½ in) protruding
Stub wires

PLANT MATERIAL
4 each dried seedheads (verbas-cum used here) and long cones
10 large green ivy leaves
10 sprigs variegated privet
4 phormium or iris leaves (looped)
7 rosettes echeveria
4 orange lilies
6 purple liatris
6 orange carnations
4 peach gerberas
Piece of dried bracket fungus
Dried cardoon head or similar

ARRANGER
Anna Sparks

1 · Place the containers close together centrally on the base board with the left-hand one raised on the hessian block and slightly back.

2 · Begin by establishing the height with two seedheads in each container at the left and to the back. The stems in the raised pot should be a little taller. Be sure the two stems in each pot are also at different heights from each other. These are important backbones to the design and need to be carefully adjusted.

3 · Wire the cones (see page 76) to give a strong stem and place two in each container, upright, on the right, so that the back one is taller than the other. Add four or five ivy leaves at the left-hand front corner.

4 · Add one tall lily to each arrangement in front of, and shorter than, the seedheads.

5 · Add clusters of privet sprigs, left, a little taller than the cones; two looped leaves beside them and three echeveria to hide the wired stems.

6 · Three liatris on the left and three orange carnations on the right strengthen the vertical block. Another lily and two gerberas, all cut quite short, complete a focal area in the front.

7 · Add a small group of dried fungus, dried flower head and an echeveria at the left-hand corner of the raised pot.

Checking the Arrangement

● This double arrangement is an interesting follow-on from the parallel grouping in European continental style on page 23. All the plant materials (there are 10 different ones in each pot) are grouped with their own kind with no intermingling, and all are placed vertically in quite rigid lines. Only the looped leaves and some of the ivy leaves give any suggestion of an outward movement. Compare it also with page 19.

The colour scheme, sometimes called *triadic*, uses three colours (with their varying tints, tones and shades) that are equally spaced round the colour wheel. The arranger chose orange (lilies, carnations, gerberas, terracotta pots and the brown seedheads and cones which are a 'shade' of orange), then purple (liatris) as an accent, and finally the varied greens of the leaves and echeveria. Triadic groupings of colours are always strong; red, blue and yellow, the three primary colours, are an example of a triadic grouping that would seem difficult to handle! In pure hues it would be, but translated into pink (tint of red), navy (shade of blue) and cream (tint of yellow), the colour scheme becomes easier to use.

Apart from the strong verticals and the colour scheme, the effectiveness of the design relies on variations and repetition of shapes and textures. The cones are needed in order to echo the shape, colour and texture of the tall seedheads. Lilies are a very different form from carnations and flat-faced gerberas, and the leaves are extremely varied. The combination of dried materials with fresh ones adds further interest.

Other Options

Using a similar format in spring-time, one could combine blue iris, cream narcissi and pink tulips (another triadic colour scheme) with various leaves. Autumn could produce bulrushes (reed-mace), gladioli and dahlias with brownish or glycerined leaves.

An alternative, sometimes called a 'mother and daughter' design has the lower placement very much shorter, perhaps only one-third the height of the taller. Individual flowers and leaves are the same size; the scaling down is in stem length and quantity.

CHAPTER THREE · REVIEW

*T*he seven concepts that make up the principles of design are always more difficult to grapple with than the design elements, which are physical qualities. Each principle may affect one of the others, and can, in turn, be affected by one or more of the elements. The permutations are infinitely variable: for example, colour can affect balance, texture can affect dominance and rhythm may reduce contrast. With practice and careful observation, however, it becomes easier to appreciate and apply these more complex relationships involved in composing an arrangement.

Balance

Visual balance is important in flower arranging. The first two pictures in this chapter show two different aspects of balance.

The tall pedestal arrangement (page 47) is symmetrically balanced about the tallest stem of pink larkspur. The two sides are not identical but they do have the same *weight* of colour. The larger bright pink roses on the left are balanced by a mass of smaller pink flowers on the right. Would a lighter-coloured column have reduced some of the bottom-heaviness, another aspect of balance?

The box (page 49) has a very gentle, almost horizontal, asymmetrical balance with curving sprays of flowering currant balancing the lower, reversed curves of rose foliage.

It is worth studying the balance of the complementary colours on page 53 to see how grouping the orange flowers (the advancing, luminous colour) highlights the supporting blues.

Proportion and Scale

Good proportion is shown in the pair of arrangements on page 55. The seedheads are tall enough to offset the width of the base and the visual weight of the terracotta containers.

The arrangements showing the principle of scale most clearly are the miniature and petite on pages 50–1. The small 'in progress' picture of the miniature shows up clearly against the white cardboard just how the scale of the plant material, of the container and of the bases must be adapted to the tiny size. The same is true of the petite. Compare the tree here with the tree on page 25.

Rhythm

The down-flowing curves of the pedestal design (page 47) and the 'S' curves in the box (page 49) create their own rhythm, and each has stems radiating clearly from the centre of the arrangement, which is another way of creating a sense of rhythm, or movement, flowing through an arrangement.

The larger design also displays attractive repetition of colour. The lime-green, which starts top-right with a branch of green snowball tree, is carried down the left side by euphorbia and the downward branch of snowballs, with just sufficient of the same colour on the right side to balance. The pink roses make a distinct line for the eye to follow from the top to below container level.

The very repetition of the twin arrangements on page 55 is rhythm in itself. The strong vertical lines, not quite matching, create an almost 'left-right' marching rhythm.

Contrast

There are two examples of contrasting, and therefore complementary, colour: in the brilliant orange and blue on page 53, and in the more gentle opposites of deep pink and green in the pedestal arrangement on page 47. These too are complementary, but the gently varied pinks and greens soften the contrasts.

Contrast in shape and in textures too is clearly evident in all five pictures.

Dominance

None of these was a show piece, so that plant material did not *have* to predominate, but in fact it does in each arrangement. The dominance of bright, or pale, luminous colours is evident in all of them, but when it comes to size are the three central roses in the box on page 49 a little too large? Or is it that the deep colour really needed to be taken out towards the upward and downward curves, either by buds or other flowers of the same strength of colour? (There was a particular problem, one that every flower arranger will recognize. The photograph was taken early in March, trying to make it look like a summer arrangement, and all the florist roses came out the same size at the same time! *Five* fully open roses would have overwhelmed everything else.)

Harmony

All the arrangements were carefully planned and the component parts thoughtfully selected. Each container, was chosen for colour, shape, texture and style with the final design clearly in mind. Where gentle lines were needed dainty plant material was chosen, and where forceful straight lines were called for seed-heads, delphiniums and larkspur were the answer. Arrangers here had new challenges: a much larger arrangement than has been shown before in the course; the opposite challenge of working in a small scale; the difficult strong, complementary colours to balance effectively; and the need to create some dominance in a pair of almost identical arrangements. And the box? Well, a Hogarth curve isn't all that easy to arrange. Try it and see.

Chapter Four

STOCKING UP
FOR WINTER

Flower arranging is not, as many think, just a summertime pleasure.
There is plenty you can do in the depths of winter, but you need to think about
stocking up supplies during the rest of the year. After the multi-colours of
spring and summer and the glowing hues of autumn,
the soft browns of many of the dried and preserved plant materials can be
enjoyed for their own sake or used as a foil for fresh or artificial flowers.

There are *three* sources of supply for winter arrangements: evergreen trees, shrubs and houseplants; dried and preserved leaves, flowers and seedheads; and artificial plant materials, which can be either home-made or chosen from the profusion now available at garden centres and florists'.

Evergreens

If you have even the smallest garden, try to plant a few evergreen shrubs to give foliage which can be cut throughout the year. Those with yellow variegation make the garden look sunny even on a cold, dull day.

Choose from the list on page 167; this includes the flower arrangers' most popular foliage plants, which are among the easiest to grow. These evergreens are not particularly fussy about soil or situation, though any variegated plant will produce more colourful foliage where there is some sun.

Drying Plant Material

Many plants can be dried for winter use and with care will last for many years. Three drying methods are described below, but all plant material for drying needs to be:
● a good undamaged specimen
● just about to reach its peak (don't waste time on over-matured flowers)
● cut and gathered on a dry day
● prepared and put to dry on the same day

Air Drying

This method is most suitable for seedheads and 'everlasting' flowers (those that retain their colour when dried). They will all dry naturally on the plant but may be damaged by rain or wind and are best harvested before then. Hang them upside-down in bunches in a dry airy place, but away from light for better colour retention. Tie the bunches so that the heads do not crush each other. Any leaves on the stalks will shrivel, so are best stripped away before drying to help speed up the drying process a little. The time taken will vary from one to four weeks.

Hydrangeas (picked when the heads begin to feel papery), gypsophila and heather dry best standing in a few centimetres (an inch or so) of water, which is not replenished as it dries out. Gourds, artichokes, oranges, lemons and pomegranates dry well in a warm place, and apples shrivel into interesting shapes.

Pressing

Pressing is suitable for flowers, petals and leaves that are of fairly thin tissue but not for bulky, fleshy flowers or those with many petals. Colour retention will be good but of course plant material is flattened to paper thinness. It may be necessary to take some flowers to pieces. For example, a daffodil should have its petals pressed separately and the trumpet cut in two and spread out for pressing. Include some stems and tendrils as they are useful for flower pictures.

A screw-down flower press with alternating layers of blotting paper and firm card is ideal for the purpose, but equally satisfactory results can be obtained by using old books or discarded telephone directories because the paper is sufficiently absorbent. They do, however, need a heavy weight on top, such as a sewing machine, bricks or a pile of heavy books, to provide enough pressure.

Choose only perfect plant specimens and take great care in laying them between the pages to avoid creases or curled-over petals. Stems can be fixed down with masking tape to give pleasing curves.

Generally speaking, smaller flowers and leaves are most useful for pictures, cards and other pressed-flower work, but, as in the pictures on pages 58 and 69, some larger flowers, such as pansies, hollyhocks, narcissi and wild roses (*Rosa canina*), can provide strong focal points in a design.

It pays to put labelling 'flags' on the sheets so you won't have to disturb the pressings unnecessarily when looking for a particular flower or leaf.

Flowers and leaves will take two to three weeks to press well this way and are best left in the press or book until needed.

Using a Microwave

The whole process can be greatly speeded up in a microwave oven. As a screw-down press must *not* be used because of the metal screws, make your own 'press' to fit the microwave tray with a firm piece of cardboard top and bottom and two sheets of newspaper and one of cardboard (cereal box cardboard is

good) alternately sandwiched between. Allow enough headroom to place a weighty pile of saucers or a brick on top of your home-made press after the plant material has been carefully put between the pieces of newspaper. Process on 'High' for two minutes. Lift out the press and weights together and *leave undisturbed for two hours* before examining the results. You'll be surprised. The work of several weeks can be condensed into a couple of hours!

Drying with Desiccants

This method is suitable for any flower but especially for those with many petals (daisies, roses, dahlias) and those with trumpet or bell shapes, as their form can be maintained. The colour retention is excellent. Desiccants – substances that can absorb moisture – most commonly used are sand, borax and silica gel.

Sand: The slowest-acting desiccant, is rather too heavy for many delicate flowers. Use silver sand if possible but it must be dried out first. Put a quantity into a large baking tin to dry out in a very slow oven for two to three hours, stirring from time to time to ensure that it is dry throughout.

Borax: Available in powder form, borax is not expensive and is one of the most popular desiccants.

Silica gel: This is the fastest-acting agent. Bought in the form of crystals, it is also obtainable from the chemist. Though expensive it can be dried out and re-used almost indefinitely. The crystals sold specifically for drying plant materials are usually the finest grade, but coarser crystals can be crushed with a rolling pin. The crystals must be quite dry (blue if tested with litmus paper) and can be dried out like sand in a slow oven. When cool they are ready to use.

Cardboard shoeboxes or plastic margarine or ice-cream boxes are convenient for the drying process. Pour a 2.5 cm (1 in) layer of desiccant into the bottom and carefully put in chosen flower heads cut with about 2.5 cm (1 in) of stem. Sift the desiccant very gently over and around each flower, filling all the crevices. Bell-shaped flowers can be filled with desiccant beforehand to help preserve their shape.

When one layer is completely covered, another can be put in in the same way. It is better to keep to one type of flower per box. Label it with the name and *date*. Leave the lid *off* the box and place it in a warm, dry place for two weeks or more (if using sand), seven to ten days (if using borax) or one to four days (if using silica gel).

Again this process can be very much speeded up in a microwave oven. Process the box for 1½ minutes on *high*. The desiccant will be very hot so leave it to cool before taking a peep at the results. Petals that have become detached can be glued back on with a clear contact adhesive, and any desiccant still clinging to the petals can be brushed gently away with a soft water-colour or make-up brush.

Adding stems: Some flowers with tough or woody stems, such as broom, rhododendron or delphinium, can be dried on their own stems. Others will need to have either wire stems added and then taped (a tricky process with fragile dried petals) or the stems from a sturdy air-dried plant glued on.

Protection: When the flowers are quite dry, they are fragile and will always need very careful handling. There are two methods of protecting desiccant-dried flowers both from dust and from re-absorbing moisture from the air. The first is to spray them with matt water-colour fixative (available in aerosol cans from artists' suppliers). The second is to dip them briefly in melted candle-wax, which gives a virtually invisible coating that protects and strengthens them. Melt the candle-wax (or household white candles) in a double boiler and dip each flower very quickly in the liquid wax. Stand it upright in a block of foam to set. It is sensible also to store stemmed flowers in this way inside a box high enough not to crush them. Add a few grains of silica gel to absorb any air moisture.

Preserving with Glycerine

Leaves, some seedheads and grasses and a few flowers can be preserved with a solution of one part glycerine to two parts hot water. It can be used while still hot. Glycerine is available from the chemist.

Anti-freeze liquid – from petrol stations and car accessory shops – may be used instead, but one-to-one proportions are better for this. Anti-freeze usually contains a colorant, which can produce some interesting results, giving red or bluish tinges to leaves.

All treated material will lose its natural colour and turn brown as glycerine is absorbed into the veins and the water in them is replaced. But this brown may vary from pale biscuit (choisya, box) to a brown that is almost black (broom), with many variations in between. The form is completely maintained and the results are tough and leathery and will last for years.

In summer, when leaves are fully mature, choose well-shaped branches and leaves and groom them carefully, cutting out all damaged leaves, re-shaping by pruning and preparing the stem end as for conditioning (pages 13–15).

Pour about 8 cm (3 in) of the glycerine solution into a glass jar – a 300 g (11 oz) coffee jar is very suitable – so that it is easy to see the level of the liquid. Place the prepared stems in the liquid, keeping the solution topped up so stem ends never dry out. Leave until the whole of the leaf or spray has turned brown, then remove it, or it may start to sweat. (If this happens, mop it with a kitchen towel, and let it dry in a warm place.) The glycerining process may take from one to three weeks.

When leaves have been glycerined they have a leathery texture and with care will last for years. But success can depend on the seasons; some are so wet the leaves get mildewed; some are so hot and dry the leaves wilt or shrivel before they can take up enough glycerine. Large leaves like aspidistra and tough ones like ivy are better submerged in the glycerine solution. Other large leaves, like fatsia, can bend at the neck and stop taking up the solution, so they need a splint to keep the neck straight.

Standing the leaves in a sunny window after they have been processed will fade them to softer, varied tones of brown.

If leaves have become dirty or dusty in use they can be washed in mild household detergent, rinsed and thoroughly dried before storing away in cardboard boxes and paper bags, rather than polythene bags, which tend to encourage sweating and mildew. Never store glycerined and air-dried materials in the same box or the moisture remaining in the glycerined plant material will ruin the others.

Wiring leaves to provide a false stem: There are two simple methods of wiring leaves.
● Lay a stub wire alongside the central vein on the back of the leaf with about 10 cm (4 in) protruding at the bottom to make a stem. Attach the wire to the back of the leaf with cellophane tape. Cover the new stem with stem-binding tape.
● Using a medium stub wire, take a small 'stitch' through the main vein about one-third up the back of the leaf. Bring the two ends of wire to the bottom. Twist one end around the other and any remaining stump of stem just twice, then lay the wires side by side and cover them with stem-binding tape.

Artificial and Made-up Flowers

For competitive work, NAFAS, and most other flower arrangement organizations, differentiate between wholly *artificial* flowers, leaves and fruits made of silk, polyester, plastic and other man-made materials, and flowers *made-up* out of natural plant materials, such as glycerined or dried leaves and seedheads, corn husks, cones, berries, nuts, etc. The artificial flowers are *not* permitted in competitive work, except perhaps at Christmas time and then only when the schedule states so. Made-up flowers are generally permitted and the unobtrusive use of wires, glue and stem-binding allowed.

BASKET OF DRIED FLOWERS

A basket of dried flowers looks pleasing in any setting whether it is a country cottage or a town flat. Baskets already arranged are expensive to buy but marvellously inexpensive, in terms of both time and money, if you can do your own. Apart from the dark brown leaf sprays of garrya and the dainty multi-flowered heads of alchemilla, all the flowers and seedheads in the basket have been dried by hanging small bunches upside-down in a dry, airy place. None is exotic and all are easy to grow.

OVERALL SIZE (W×H)
90×50 cm (36×20 in)

YOU WILL NEED
Shallow basket with handle, about 40×30 cm (16×12 in)
20 cm (8 in) plastic flower-pot saucer or pet's ceramic feeding bowl
A few stones or pieces of lead for weight (optional), putty-type adhesive or plasticine (optional)

MECHANICS
Block of dry foam (brown) to fit saucer and 8 cm (3 in) high
Sticky tape

PLANT MATERIAL
Dried: dock (rumex), achillea, seedheads of poppy (papaver) and teazel (Dipsacus fullonum), cones, larch sprays, wheat, barley, heads of artichoke and allium
Glycerined: garrya leaves, alchemilla flowers

ARRANGER
Betty Shewring

1 · Get into the habit of working on a sheet of polythene or newspaper. Dried materials shed seeds and bits all the time and this will save you a lot of sweeping up afterwards. The basket looks most attractive seen from above, so put

it on a low table or chair to work at the right angle. Place the long side of the basket towards you but slightly on the diagonal, so that the front and back curves of the handle show, as in the picture.

2 · Strap the block of dry foam into the plant saucer or bowl and stand it in the centre of the basket. If a plastic saucer is being used, it will be very lightweight and unstable so add a few stones or pieces of lead to weight it down. Alternatively, secure the bowl to the basket with putty-type adhesive or plasticine.

3 · Start by establishing the length with stems of dock, larch sprays or poppy, pushing them low down into the *sides*, not the top, of the foam. This leaves room for the central, more upright stems to be added later.

4 · Now establish the height, being sure to leave the handle showing, and also the width using shorter stems such as the wheat and barley, cones (see page 76 for wiring), and alchemilla. Take some over the sides of the basket to disguise the hard line of the basket rim.

5 · Insert garrya sprays to fill out the corners, using the shorter sprigs to cover some of the foam.

The darker colour will give more depth to the arrangement. The alchemilla flowers also provide an excellent means of covering the foam.

6 · Now the stronger, bolder shapes can go in on shorter (but not too short) stems. The flat yellow heads of achillea, domed teazels, bunches of wired cones, artichoke heads and rounded alliums give shape and form to the arrangement.

Checking the Arrangement

● As the basket will be looked into from above, any large areas of foam need some covering, but beware of stuffing in too many

stems. It can look too packed and muddled if you do.

● Because leaves shrivel as they dry out, the stems of most dried flowers and seedheads are bare and arrangements can look very stalky unless some glycerine-preserved leaves are used. The alternative is to use *pressed* leaves that have been wired to provide a stem if necessary (see page 61). Pressed bracken or ferns are useful, as are the pressed leaves of acer, ivy, laurel, rhododendron.

● When using a handled basket allow the handle to show; there is no point otherwise in choosing it as a container. Ideally it should look as if it can be picked up without crushing the contents or scratching one's hand.

Other Options

The arranger here used materials that were available in her own or her friends' gardens. There are, obviously, many alternatives, and for the arranger seeking to grow plants for drying there are many, many possibilities. Consider any of the following:

Everlastings, also called immortelles, are flowers which dry without losing their summer colour. They include acroclinum, achillea (used here), love-lies-bleeding (amaranthus), globe amaranth, lavender, pearly everlasting (anaphalis), strawflower (helichrysum), rhodanthe, sea lavender (statice), xeranthemum (common immortelle).

Seedheads that can be hung to dry with a minimum of fuss include acanthus, allium, artichoke, bulrush, foxglove (digitalis), globe thistle (*Echinops ritro*), iris (including the orange-berried *I. foetidissima*), nicandra, love-in-the-mist (nigella), honesty (lunaria), teazel and Chinese lantern or Cape gooseberry (physalis).

Grasses nearly all dry well if picked while they are still silky and not too dry. The huge plumes of pampas (cortaderia) are especially popular. The same applies to old man's beard, the name for the hairy seedheads of wild clematis (*Clematis vitalba*), and the furry catkins of pussy willow (*Salix caprea*).

STUDY IN BROWN

One of the most useful and versatile stores for winter use is a collection of leaves and seedheads preserved with glycerine. Chosen wisely they can be used over and over again in different arrangements, with either air-dried, fresh or artificial materials or a combination of all three. The subtle tints, tones and shades of brown that the glycerine solution produces cover a very wide range, from the palest biscuit to virtually black, with tans, mid-browns, and greyish browns in between. They look best with white, yellow and orange flowers and can provide a foil for paler blues and pinks.

OVERALL SIZE (W×H)
76×90 cm (30×36 in)

YOU WILL NEED
Low bowl 15–18 cm (6–7 in) in diameter
Circular base, 25 cm (10 in) in diameter, covered in neutral matt fabric

MECHANICS
Half-brick dry foam (brown)
Large 'frog' to anchor it
Putty-type adhesive

PLANT MATERIAL
Yucca leaves (dried and split vertically)
Glycerined: crocosmia seedheads, eucalyptus, ruscus, single Mahonia japonica leaves
3 types of made-up flowers: 'gladioli' made from corn husks (see method); flowers made of star-shaped petals cut from coconut fibre, with cone centre (bought); flowers made of curled wood shavings with cone centre (bought)
Artificial flowers: 10 creamy 'roses', from buds to fully open flowers

ARRANGER
Gwen Mason

1 · Fix the 'frog' in the bowl and impale the dry foam on it.

2 · The height is established by the spike of 'gladioli' made out of the cream-coloured outer husks of sweet corn. Petals are cut out to resemble gladiolus flowers and four or five are wired together and onto a central stub wire or dried stem. The flowers are larger lower down and smaller, like closed buds, at the top.

3 · This 'backbone' stem is backed up by the yucca leaves, stems of crocosmia seedheads and eucalyptus.

4 · The side stems are of eucalyptus and ruscus; those on the right are longer, coming forward over the corner of the table, so that a slightly asymmetrical balance is created.

5 · This is balanced on the left by larger and darker mahonia leaves and the star-shaped made-up flowers.

6 · Eucalyptus leaves, ruscus and the wood-shavings flowers are used to fill in.

7 · Lastly add the creamy artificial flowers that look like roses.

Checking the Arrangement

● The round shape of the artificial flowers is important as a contrast to the longer, spiky sprays of leaves. The buds go to the top and the line curves down in a loose, reversed 'S' shape to the edge of the table.
● If a picture hangs near an arrangement, make sure it is not obscured by leaves or flowers.
● The golden-beige wall, apricot curtains and dark mahogany table make a fine setting for this study in brown and the whitish flowers make a link with the white-painted dado.

Other Options

The list of plants on page 73 for preserving gives many that could be used instead of those in the photograph. As with the foliage arrangement on page 33, where the colour range is virtually monochromatic, it is the variety of size, shape and texture that creates the interest. You can mix dried and glycerined material as available, though desiccant-dried materials are usually kept apart as they can so quickly absorb moisture from glycerined leaves and seedheads.

COLOURFUL DRIED FLOWERS

It is hard to believe that this fresh-looking arrangement is entirely of dried flowers! Each one has been dried, given a false stem where needed and had its petals glued back on if they shattered in the drying process. The elegant mixture of spring, summer and autumn flowers is in the style of the great Dutch masters, who used their sketchbook studies to make painted arrangements that included flowers of all seasons. The arranger has gone one better, making an arrangement which is just as colourful, but is the real thing. The flowers here have all been dried in borax, one of the desiccants described on page 60.

OVERALL SIZE (W×H)
60×76 cm (24×30 in)

YOU WILL NEED
Cardboard shoeboxes, plastic food boxes
Longer boxes for long sprays
Household borax from the chemist: approximately two 1kg (2 lb) packets for each shoebox
Matt water-colour fixative spray (from artists' suppliers)
Raised container or urn on a plinth

MECHANICS
Block of dry foam to fit container

PLANT MATERIAL
Flowers: delphiniums in two shades of blue, pink larkspur, sprays of bridal wreath (Spiraea x arguta), which is white when fresh, but turns a pleasing cream as it dries, parrot and other tulips, daffodils, hellebores, anemones, carnations, crocosmia, roses, dark red peonies, bells of Ireland (molucella), fuchsias, 1 purple auricula
Leaves: alchemilla, jasmine, ivy, epimedium, thalictrum

ARRANGER
Dallas Taylor

1 · The flowers and leaves need to be dried over a period of months. It is essential that they are picked at their peak of freshness and quite dry from morning dew or rain before being put into borax. Cut off the stems of single flowers to about 5 cm (2 in).

2 · Put a 2.5 cm (1 in) layer of borax in a suitable-sized box, lay in the flower heads (not touching) and gently sift over more borax to fill all the crevices and cover them completely. Bell-shaped flowers should be filled with borax to keep their shape before being laid in the box. The delphiniums and longer sprays are dried in long boxes.

3 · Leave the filled boxes, uncovered, in a warm, dry place for seven to ten days. The length of time needed is a matter of trial and error, but a flower can always be put back for longer treatment if necessary. Flowers should feel papery to the touch when they are ready.

4 · When emptying the box, do so very gently, over newspaper, and lift the flowers out with care. They will be fragile and always need careful handling. They will still be covered with a dusting of borax which can be brushed off with a small make-up or paint brush.

5 · Fallen petals can be glued back in place with a clear contact adhesive, such as Dunlop Thixofix. Peonies usually lose all their petals, but the lengthy job of gluing them back is well worth it. Before flowers are used, spray them with a matt water-colour fixative, which protects and strengthens them. Dried flowers can be glued into dried hollow stems from other flowers or given a wire stem if a curve is needed.

6 · When you have enough dried flowers to arrange (they are unlikely to be exactly the ones used here) fit a block of dry foam into a raised container, which will allow for some downward-flowing stems. With no need for a water supply, stems can be lengthened as needed. For guidance on arranging the flowers, look back to pages 32–5.

7 · There will not be many leaves to help cover the mechanics, and dried arrangements can look 'stemmy' because of this, so use shorter flowers to mask long, bare stems.

8 · Because the colours of dried plant materials do fade over time, it is better not to stand a finished arrangement in sunlight or too near a window.

Checking the Arrangement

● With a polychromatic arrangement like this, using many different sorts of flowers, the balance of colour from top to bottom and from side to side is important.
● Note how the dark blue delphinium is balanced by the black-based container and the purple auricula, with the red and orange tulips balanced right and left.

Other Options

Working with desiccant-dried flowers requires, above all, patience and the willingness to experiment. Don't be discouraged if attempts end in failure: try again or try a different desiccant.

The flower may have been damp, or immature, or past its best. You may have left it in the desiccant too long, or not long enough.

The style of arrangement shown here is traditional, but the arrangements can, of course, be in any style. Arrangers use

florets to decorate cards and gift boxes, and flowers and leaves to make swags also using dried material (but not material preserved in glycerine as it can sweat and provide too moist an atmosphere). Miniaturists use them for small treasures.

PRESSED FLOWER PICTURE

Pressed flower pictures, large or small, have all the fascination of scrapbooks and are far more decorative. They can record, in pictorial form, the delights of a spring or summer garden or a wedding bouquet. Flowers and leaves picked and pressed on a special holiday can be made into a permanent souvenir, and as gifts for friends pictures have a personal touch no bought present can equal. Pressed flowers do not take up much storage space and offer many possibilities for flower-craft even for those who have only a small flat and no garden.

OVERALL SIZE (W × H)
*Including frame 50 × 60 cm
(20 × 24 in)*

YOU WILL NEED
*Oval gilt frame, picture glass to fit
1 sheet black paper
Stiff cardboard backing
PVA adhesive such as Marvin
Medium or Child's Play
Cocktail sticks/toothpicks
Small, pointed scissors, tweezers
Small, shallow pot or jar
Brown paper*

PLANT MATERIAL
*Pressed flowers and florets in
white, cream and yellow (if
possible including 2 large white
hollyhock flowers); stems and
leaves, buttercups, lawn daisies,
Queen Anne's lace, astrantia
and ferns*

ARRANGER
Betty James

1 · It is always sensible to choose a frame first and then compose a picture to fit it, rather than the other way around. Cut the black paper to fit inside the frame and note how much of it will be covered by the frame. Allow enough margin space when composing the picture so that the plant material does not look squashed in or get hidden behind the picture frame.

2 · Begin designing the picture by laying out the pressed materials on the paper. Unlike a 3–D flower arrangement, where it is usual to start with an outline, here it is better to start with the largest focal flower and work out from there. *Glue nothing at this stage.* The largest flowers here are the two white hollyhocks, and they have Queen Anne's lace florets in the centre as 'stamens'. The hollyhocks are just off-centre with one above and to the right. Pansies would make a good alternative, or rose petals re-composed into a flower and given a new centre.

3 · Group medium-sized flowers such as buttercups, narcissi and daisies around the central flowers. Cut and trim them as necessary. Choose stems for the bottom of the bouquet.

4 · Build up the pattern with smaller flowers, leaves, ferns and buds to make a balanced, but not rigidly symmetrical, group. In the picture the colouring is kept to white, cream, yellow and beige which is shown off well by the black background and links with the gilt frame.

5 · When you are satisfied with the design, it is time to start sticking. Pour a little of the adhesive into the pot and use a cocktail stick to apply small spots to the underside of each piece of plant material. It is not necessary to use much adhesive – just enough to keep each item in place.

6 · Where petals, leaves or stalks will overlap another piece, judge whether it is necessary to cut away from underneath to avoid an unsightly ridge; there are no rules. When the picture is complete, leave it for 24 hours to set.

7 · Clean the glass thoroughly, especially on the inside. Place the glass carefully over the picture and put it inside the frame. Lay the picture face downwards and put on the cardboard backing. Cut the brown paper ever so slightly smaller than the outer circumference of the frame and glue it firmly over the back to keep out dust.

8 · When the picture is hung it should not be in full light from the window or on a sunny wall, as the colours will fade quickly.

Checking the Arrangement

● The picture shown here was photographed without the glass for greater clarity, but to last well these delicate pictures should be glazed. The more firmly the glass presses down, the better the plant materials are preserved. An alternative seal, especially for greetings cards, is a clear, self-adhesive polythene sheet.
● The background paper or fabric (either can be used) should not be too heavily textured as it will show through thin flower petals. Some interest can be added, however, by using Ingres, marbled or manila papers or by using a colour-wash, perhaps suggesting a sky.

Other Options

Pressed-flower picture designs can be endlessly varied: a simple spray, a curving crescent, a pattern of leaves, a wreath or garland, a geometric pattern, a hedgerow frieze, meadow flowers in a basket (made from fern or bracken fronds) – the possibilities are endless. Colours can be delicate and pastel or richly polychromatic. As some colours fade quite quickly, even in poor light, you may like to add artificial colour to counteract this process. Use children's water-soluble felt pens, and spread the colour evenly with a moistened cotton bud or finger. As flowers and leaves are very brittle, care and patience are needed.

PRESSED LEAF COLLAGE

A collage carried out in plant materials is a recent development of the pressed-flower picture in which the flowers, leaves and stems are used in a naturalistic manner. In the collage pictured here, although the scene portrayed is a natural one, the plant material is used in an abstract way simply for its colour, shape or texture. For the most part, pressed leaves have been used with some seeds and seedheads. The shape of leaves is not always important as pieces can be cut from them if they are the right colour and texture.

OVERALL SIZE (W×H)
Picture 48×32 cm (19×12½ in); framed and mounted 58×43 cm (23×17 in)

YOU WILL NEED
Sheet of pale cream Ingres paper
Mounting board
Frame (or have it framed professionally)

TOOLS
2B pencil with a sharp point
Small, sharp craft knife
Embroidery scissors
Water-based white glue
Cutting board to work on
Pastel chalks, aerosol fixative

PLANT MATERIALS
Pressed leaves and seedheads (those used are listed by the plan)

ARRANGER
Betty Scall

1 · With the Ingres paper on a firm flat surface, pencil in lightly the main outlines of the picture, such as the horizon, position and size of the buildings, roadway, large tree and thatched ricks. Details of distant hills, clumps of trees and the foreground can be composed as the picture progresses.

2 · Using pastels, tint the sky and roadway. Take the colouring over the pencilled guidelines, as later glued-on materials will cover this. Spray the pastels with the fixative.

3 · Select pressed leaves for the main features, cut them out, and lay them in position *without* sticking them down. When satisfied with the choice and placing, glue them in place with adhesive in the centre. Leave the edges free in case they need trimming or lifting to tuck another leaf underneath.

4 · Continue with the fields, trees, hedges and distant hills and add foliage to the tree on the right, composing as you go along.

5 · Now add the details of shading, gate posts, house door and windows, birds, and extra shrubs, where needed. The poppy seedheads, sprinkled on to a little pool of adhesive, will make interesting shadows.

6 · The picture may finally need touching up with pastel, for example in the shadows and on the thatching, to give form and depth. If you need to spray later pastel work, mask the plant material when doing so, or the fixative will add a shiny finish.

Checking the Arrangement

● You may find it helpful to try out a small practice picture first. Make an outline sketch from a landscape picture or photograph. You will then begin to appreciate the details that must be omitted, the importance of texture in choice of plant material and some of the possibilities of composition.
● Before mounting and framing, this picture was heat-sealed, a professional finish offered by many picture-framers or photographers. The cost is roughly comparable with having the picture glazed. This is an irrevocable process, however, whereas a picture framed under glass can, if wished, be dismantled and altered.

Other Options

This type of collage opens up many possibilities. For example, you can mix the technique used here with naturalistic small flowers and grasses in a landscape scene.

Alternatively, wholly abstract patterns and compositions are possible using a blend of pressed and preserved flowers and leaves, pieces of bark, seeds, fungus and so on.

A few poppy and grass seeds have been used in this picture, but whole collages can be done in just seed alone. There is a wonderful range of colour – including pearly-white rice, green split peas, orange lentils, striped sunflower seeds, black hosta seeds and brown apple and grape pips – and of size, from tiny poppy seeds to large, wrinkled peach stones.

Seed collages usually need to be in recessed frames because of their thickness, but it is often possible just to varnish them rather than actually cover them with glass.

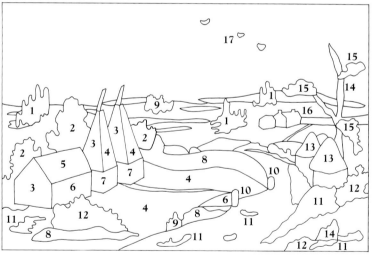

PLANT MATERIALS USED HERE

All are leaves except where stated.
G = glycerined before pressing

1 Astilbe seedheads
2 Aquilegia
3 New Zealand flax, sheaths of flowers
4 Aspidistra
5 Tulip

6 Autumn crocus
7 Globe thistle, front and back (G)
8 Arum
9 Ladder fern leaflets (G)
10 Aucuba (G)
11 Poppy seeds
12 Thalictrum
13 Seeds of horsetail grass
14 Amaryllis

15 Green reindeer moss
16 Front of house – Eleagnus ebbingii (G)
   Roof – back of echinops leaf
   Gable end – front of echinops leaf
17 Birds cut from fern frondlets

Undulations of distant hills and fields cut from tulip leaves of different colours

CHAPTER FOUR · REVIEW

*E*vergreens can be used throughout the year to add variety to flower arrangements. Artificial and made-up flowers extend the possibilities even more. Drying and preserving flowers, leaves, seedheads and fruits as they become ripe for harvesting in spring, summer and autumn, provides the flower arranger with a store to match the cook's convenience foods. 'Recipes' for using them are set out in this chapter and in Chapter 5.

Methods of Preserving

There are several methods of drying and preserving plant material, and usually one method is more suitable than the others for a particular flower, leaf or seedhead.

Air drying is the easiest and most reliable method, calling for no special equipment, but enough space to dry bunches in a warm, dry atmosphere, preferably in the dark or in dim light. Generally the form is kept, and much of the colour, though brightness will be lost, except in helichrysums. Use for everlasting flowers and for seedheads and fruits.

Pressing suits flowers and leaves that are of thinner, less robust structure. Paper-thin petals press well. The form, of course, is flattened but colour will be maintained, though some colours darken. Special flower presses may be bought, but old telephone directories, with a weight on top, work just as well. Failures are few if the material is arranged carefully to avoid creases and overlapping.

Desiccant drying calls for patience and nimble fingers but can have superb results, retaining form and almost all the colours of the fresh flower. The cost is not prohibitive either, if household borax is used. Silica-gel crystals are rather more expensive but can be dried out and re-used repeatedly. Plant material dried in this way is fragile and can re-absorb moisture from the air, so it needs careful treatment in use and in storage.

Preserving with glycerine is the only really effective method of preserving relatively thick leaves, including most of the evergreens. The form is kept and the leaves are generally quite leathery, but the natural colour is lost and turns to a brown tint or shade. Glycerine is quite expensive and the solution can be used effectively only once, or maybe twice, so be selective in what you try to preserve.

Selecting Materials

Do not waste time (and money) trying to preserve materials not in perfect peak condition.

Try to ensure that you are preserving or drying, by one means or another, some of each of the three shapes referred to on page 27: long, narrow outline material, intermediate and bushy material, and rounded 'points'. With these available an arrangement is at once possible. Preserving for arrangements in the home also means you know which containers you are likely to use and where they will stand, so select plant material with this in mind.

Plants for Preserving

AIR-DRYING	PRESSING	DESICCANT DRYING	PRESERVING WITH GLYCERINE
EVERLASTING	FLOWERS	FLOWERS	LEAVES/SPRAYS
Achillea	*Astrantia*	*Anemone*	*Aspidistra*
Acroclinum	*Buttercup*	*Auricula*	*Bay*
Amaranthus	*Crocosmia*	*Camellia*	*Beech*
Globe amaranth	*Daisy*	*Campanula*	*Box*
Globe thistle	*Daffodil (cut down)*	*Carnation*	*Broom*
Helichrysum	*Elder*	*Clematis*	*Camellia*
Helipterum	*Forget-me-not*	*Daffodil*	*Choisya*
Lavender	*Fressia*	*Dahlia*	*Cupressus*
Pearly everlasting (anaphalis)	*Grasses*	*Delphinium*	*Eleagnus*
Rhodanthe	*Hellebore*	*Freesia*	*Eucalyptus*
Statice	*Hollyhock*	*Hellebore*	*Garrya*
Xeranthemum (common immortelle)	*Mimosa*	*Hollyhock*	*Laurel*
	Narcissus	*Larkspur*	*Magnolia*
OTHERS	*Pansy*	*Lily*	*Mahonia*
Acanthus	*Potentilla*	*Narcissus*	*Oak*
Allium	*Primrose*	*Orchid*	*Rosemary*
Bulrush	*Queen Anne's lace*	*Pansy*	*Skimmia*
Cereals – oats, wheat, rye, barley	*Rose (petals)*	*Peony*	*Whitebeam (sorbus)*
Chinese lantern (physalis)	LEAVES	*Rose*	CATKINS
Cones	*Acer (Autumn colours)*	*Snowdrop*	*Willow (salix)*
Delphinium	*Beech*	*Tulip*	*Garrya*
Eryngium	*Bramble*	*and many more*	*Hazel*
Fungi (bracket)	*Cupressus*	LEAVES	FLOWERS
Grasses (inc pampas)	*Ferns*	*Grey leaves*	*Alchemilla*
Heather	*Grey leaves*		*Eryngium*
Hydrangea	STEMS		*Hydrangea*
Honesty (lunaria)	*Buttercup*		*Bells of Ireland (molucella)*
Iris pods	*Clematis*		SEEDHEADS
Love-in-a-mist (nigella)	*Primrose*		*Antirrhinum*
Nicandra	TENDRILS		*Atriplex*
Peony seedheads	*Clematis*		*Foxglove (digitalis)*
Poppy seedheads	*Sweetpea*		*Dock (rumex)*
Teazel	*Vine*		*Clematis (while silky)*
FRUITS			
Apple			
Lemon			
Lime			
Orange			
Pineapple (small)			
Pomegranate			
Sweetcorn			

Chapter Five

WREATHS, GARLANDS, SWAGS AND TREES

Although made-up 'topiary' trees are relative newcomers to the decorative scene, swags, garlands and wreaths are among the oldest forms of flower decoration. They go back at least to the times of Ancient Egypt many centuries before Christ. Unhappily, the term 'wreath' has come to mean, for many people, a circular garland for funerals, and even now, when Christmas wreaths are so popular, many prefer to call them rings or garlands rather than wreaths. Yet they have always been a symbol of eternity and rebirth and were part of joyful celebrations in the past. They deserve to be used more often today.

arlands, swags and wreaths are specialized forms of floral decoration with no obvious container and it is often forgotten that they are still 'flower arrangements'. They are as useful today as in classical times, and inspiration can be found in painting, tapestries and carvings in wood, plaster and stone.

The original inspiration for 'topiary' trees came from garden topiary, where shrubs and trees were clipped into shapes ranging from the simple to the fantastic. From Renaissance times on, these real trees have been brought indoors . But the copying of these and of natural tree shapes in made-up decorations does not date from earlier than the 20th century.

Wreaths

For wreaths – which are really a circular type of garland – you can buy mechanics of various types in different sizes. The main sorts are: floral foam in a round plastic trough; dry (brown) foam in ready-cut circles; polystyrene rings for wired and artificial stems; wire frames for packing with moss. You can also buy ready-made rings of bound twigs, plaited and twisted vines or stems, woven cane or packed straw.

It is much cheaper to make your own versions of these (see page 84) if you are able to get hold of vines, straw, wistaria or contorted or weeping willow. It sometimes helps to use a wire coat-hanger pulled into a roughly circular shape as a base on which to start, covering it as you twine and bind. Cut off the hook first and make a smaller loop, with which to hang it, as this will be more easily hidden.

Garlands

Garlands are long and flexible enough to wind around a column or along a mantelpiece or banister. Various mechanics for these are possible. They are described in 'A Garland of Fresh Flowers' (see page 80). They all work well, but such factors as position, length, width and cost all need to be considered when choosing which mechanics to use. For a dried garland, wiring is essential; it can be constructed like the 'Grinling Gibbons Swag' on page 76.

Just when a garland becomes a swag is never quite clear. For competitive work the *NAFAS Handbook of Schedule Definitions* (8th edition) defines them thus: 'Garland: an exhibit in which all components are assembled in an elongated and/or flexible design with no visible background.'

'Swag: an exhibit designed to hang, in which all components are assembled without a visible background.'

For non-competitive work – for example, at festivals, in stately homes and in churches – there are absolutely no hard-and-fast rules.

Swags

There are two essentially different types of swag: the *horizontal festoon*, which is suspended at each end and hangs in a gentle curve; and the *vertical cluster*, which is suspended from the top. The latter may be rectangular, triangular, circular, oval or in two or three parts spaced out on cord or ribbon. The swag described on page 76 combines both horizontal and vertical features. The mechanics for a swag are described on page 78.

Inspiration can come from paintings and tapestries, carvings in stately homes and the work of the 17th-century British woodcarver, Grinling Gibbons, and the 18th-century British architect/designer Robert Adam. Fresh or dried materials can be used, and ribbons, cords, cherubs, shells, bows, toys, etc can be included when appropriate to the setting.

Trees

The basis of virtually all topiary trees is a 'trunk' set in cement, plaster of paris or cellulose filler in a plastic flower pot or food tin. At first ribbon-bound or painted dowelling was used for trunks, or broom handles for larger trees. Then natural tree branches such as apple, silver birch or curving vine were deemed more attractive. Trunks with branches or trunks made from several thinner ones glued together make good variations.

When deciding what to use for the trunk and for the base pot/tin, make sure that the trunk is of sufficient thickness that the tree will not look top-heavy. Also, remember that you will almost certainly stand the base inside an outer pot, cache-pot, urn or basket, so the relative proportions of outer container, trunk and tree head should be pleasing.

The tree heads can be balls of dry or wet foam impaled on the trunk (two nails driven through at right angles will prevent the foam from slipping down). They need not be perfect spheres as the plant material will cover them. A sphere made from 2.5 cm (1 in) wire mesh and packed with leftover pieces of foam or moss may be used instead.

If evergreens are to cover the tree, then try to use long-lasting, bushy types such as box or cupressus, or those which form a rosette of leaves such as choisya, laurustinus, holly, hebe, skimmia and tree ivy, as they have greater covering capacity.

Because trees can be any size, all kinds of plant materials can be used for them. Hydrangea heads or separate florets have an excellent covering capacity, and so has achillea. Helichrysums make a colourful top. Silver honesty 'pennies' can be wired in clusters as can beech nut cases. Once you have tried your hand at one or two, ideas will come thick and fast.

GRINLING GIBBONS SWAG

The exquisite swags and garlands of Grinling Gibbons, Master Carver in Wood to King Charles II at the end of the 17the century, have provided inspiration for many flower arrangers working with dried and preserved plant materials. Gibbons worked from nature, carving leaves, flowers and fruits, mainly in lime wood. The arranger emulates these wood carvings and, like Gibbons, often includes cherubs, ribbons, shells, birds and even musical instruments in these decorations.

OVERALL SIZE (W×H)
The centre curve is 102 cm (40 in) long and the vertical drops 66 cm (26 in).

YOU WILL NEED
Reel, stub and silver rose wires
Wire cutters
Brown stem-binding tape (either plastic or waxed paper)
Cotton sheeting
Fabric stiffener or wallpaper paste
Matt black paint
Gold paint or spray
Tube of gold paste such as 'Gold finger' (from artists' suppliers)
Wood drill with a fine bit

PLANT MATERIAL
Cones: cedar, pine, fir, spruce
Walnuts, cob nuts in sheaths
Poppy seedheads
Small gourds, eucalyptus pods
Dried oranges, lemons
Lotus seedheads and their seeds
Lychees (for 'strawberries')
Fresh strawberry leaves dipped in fabric stiffener
Dried seedheads resembling flowers

ACCESSORIES
Scallop shells

ARRANGER
Shirley Monckton

1 · The first task is to wire all the plant material to give it a false stem that can be curved and bent. Some, such as gourds, nuts, dried fruit, shells, will have to be drilled to get a wire through. Cones can be wired by pushing a stub wire down into the lower scales and bringing the two ends together by the natural stem. Twist the ends once then tape them lying side by side. All wire stems should be taped so that when pressed together in the long garland they adhere and do not slip.

2 · To make a fabric bow or 'tails' for the end of the drops, tear off a long strip of cotton sheeting and dip it in fabric stiffener in a basin, or paint it on with a brush, or just spread it on with your hands. Tie and model the bow while wet and set it aside to dry thoroughly. Alternatively, soak the fabric in thick wallpaper paste and mould it in the same way.

3 · It is now possible to paint or spray everything gold, but to get a really antique look, paint everything *black* first, including the bow and 'tails', and let it dry. Now paint or spray with gold, but not heavily, leaving black in some parts and crevices for the aged look. When dry again, touch up the highlights with the gold paste, rubbing it on with your finger or a small pad of fabric.

4 · To assemble the swag, bind one stem to the next with binding tape, keeping the stem wires parallel to each other. Don't twist them together, as this makes a clumsy job. Each new piece or cluster gradually covers the stems of the earlier ones. Because everything is wired, there is no danger of stems breaking and each piece can be coaxed and bent into the best position.

5 · Make the vertical drops separately. Start with the fabric tails and overlap the plant materials and their stems till the desired length is almost reached, then incorporate the bow and use some of the wire stems to make a loop for attaching to the main swag. The two drops should look balanced but they need not actually be identical.

6 · An alternative method of making the swag is to bind the plant material to a cord or rope. A thick wire can be used instead of a rope, but it does not give quite the same natural bend.

7 · Finally touch up any pieces that need more gold or add something if a gap appears.

Checking the Arrangement

Once the swag is hung, check that the two curves look balanced and equal in thickness and that the two drops are equal in length and taper gently.

Other Options

Aim at a variety of shapes and textures, but if trying to achieve the 'Gibbons' effect, keep the plant materials fairly bold. Grinling Gibbons' swags and 'trophies', as the wall panels were called, were never fussy, in spite of his meticulous attention to detail.

If you want the swag to look like natural wood, omit all the painting, except perhaps a little varnish for highlights.

A very different effect can be achieved by painting everything white to emulate swags carved in stone, marble or plaster. Several coats may be needed. A lighter and more delicate swag can suggest the work of Robert Adam.

A FRESH SWAG

When garden roses are at their peak in summer, a most attractive hanging decoration is a swag of fresh flowers and leaves, bringing all the scent of summer indoors. If well-conditioned beforehand, the swag will last for at least a week and the roses as they fade and shatter can be replaced with fresh ones. Once the mechanics, which are explained here, have been mastered, swags can be made of any fresh plant material. They do not necessarily have to hang, but can lie instead on a flat surface or grace a dining table or a mantelpiece.

OVERALL SIZE (W × H)
40 × 90 cm (16 × 36 in)

YOU WILL NEED
Strip of wood or hardboard
10 × 45 cm (4 × 18 in)

MECHANICS
Block of soaked floral foam
Cling film
Piece of 2.5 cm (1 in) wire mesh
60 × 25 cm (24 × 10 in)
Stub wires
Nylon fishing line, to hang
Wire cutters, hand-drill

PLANT MATERIAL
Sprays green privet
Green ivy leaves
20 roses (used here are 'Albertine' and 'The Flower Arranger')
1–2 stems lilies
3 stems alstroemeria
A few stems alchemilla

ARRANGER
Caroline Nash

In olden days, swags of fresh flowers and leaves would have been made on a rope, with no water supply. Water-retaining foams have made it possible for present-day swags to last much longer.

1 · Drill two holes at the top of the board and make a stub-wire loop for hanging.

2 · Slice the soaked foam block horizontally to make two 22 × 10 × 4 cm (9 × 4 × 1½ in) blocks. Wrap each in cling film, taking folds and thickness to back. Lay them on the wood strip and cover the whole thing with wire mesh, securing at the back with stub wires.

3 · Work on a flat surface covered with polythene sheeting but hold up the swag from time to time to see it as it will hang. Begin by inserting sprays of privet to establish the overall length and width and to start making a framework for the flowers by covering the foam. Use the ivy leaves to finish obscuring the mechanics, but avoid packing them so closely that the flower stems cannot be inserted.

4 · Set aside six of the largest and most fully open roses, which will be needed for the centre of the swag. Use buds and half-open roses to fill in between the foliage, tapering towards the top and bottom and making sure that the flowers are taken around to the sides. Use the largest roses as shown in the main picture opposite.

5 · To provide some variation of flower shape, add a few alstroemeria florets and single heads cut from the lilies. Sprigs of alchemilla make a feathery contrast to the smooth green leaves. Mist spray the swag before hanging.

6 · With the wire loop at the back the swag may be hung in any suitable position using nylon fishing line, which is virtually invisible. Tie the line firmly with three knots, as nylon tends to slip. Be prepared for the swag to drip for a while as excess water in the foam drains out. Put a towel or folded newspaper underneath to catch the drips. If it is necessary to protect the wall from wire scratches or water, cut a strip of thick polythene and glue it to the top of the base board.

Checking the Arrangement

The essential point about a swag is that no base or prepared background shows; these are simply mechanics to provide support and, when needed (as here), a water supply.

Other Options

There are many variations on this theme at all times of the year. Spring bulb flowers can have cupressus and evergreen foliage intermixed. In autumn, fruits, berries and foliage need no flowers added. Winter evergreens with holly berries and cones – perhaps touched with gold, or with white paint or glitter to look frosted – make a long-lasting decoration.

The shape can be varied too; it can have a wide top tapering to a point at the bottom, or it can be 'waisted' to give wider and narrower sections. Accessories may include ribbons as bows or cross-gartering, shells, cherubs, baubles, feathers and so on as the occasion demands.

The 'mechanics' photograph below shows a smaller wooden board prepared for the green swag shown in the picture at the bottom right of the page. The larger swag is built up on a wire frame, which the arranger had found to be suitable, though most people will have easier access to a strip of hardboard or wood.

The green swag shown below is about 45 cm (18 in) long and uses the same type of mechanics, but it lies on a flat surface. The iris leaves at one end and the green corn stalks at the other establish the length. Fatsia leaves, large ivy leaves, lonicera and blue spruce make the width. Central interest comes from lime-green alchemilla and the large round seed heads of Jerusalem sage (*Phlomis fruticosa*).

GARLAND OF FRESH FLOWERS

The essential difference between a garland and the swag described on the previous page is its flexibility. A garland can twine around things (a pillar, statue, banister) or hang horizontally in a gentle curve with vertical drops. It can be fat or slender and made just with foliage, flowers, berries and fruits, or dried and preserved leaves and seedheads. Although various mechanics are possible for a garland, the one described here is generally the most popular because it is so adaptable in width and length.

OVERALL SIZE (W×H)
107×20 cm (42×8 in)

YOU WILL NEED

MECHANICS
Block of soaked floral foam
Cling film
Reel and stub wires, wire cutters
Piece of 2.5 cm (1 in) wire mesh

PLANT MATERIAL
Variety of short sprigs of cupressus, pieris (new pink tips if possible), red berberis, variegated privet, choisya
15 pink roses
10 clusters 'Ballerina' roses
4 stems creamy-yellow spray chrysanthemums
Dill/gypsophila/Queen Anne's lace

ARRANGER
Annette Stoker

1 · Cut the soaked foam block in half lengthwise, then cut each piece in half, then each of those into thirds, making 12 small blocks each measuring 11.5×3.5 ×4 cm (4½×1½×1¼ in). Wrap the blocks in cling film in pairs with a wire twist between each. For an indoor garland, allow the blocks to drain before use.

2 · Cover each pair with wire mesh then join as many as needed with reel wire and gently bend to the approximate curve needed. Tie off each end and leave a length of wire to be used for hanging. The large wooden curtain rings, 8 cm (3 in) in diameter, in the picture can be used with an indoor garland if a lighter, more spacious effect is needed. You will need an extra small screw-eye to each ring to be able to wire them into the garland. One ring alternating with two foam blocks looks good.

3 · It is easier to work on a flat surface, as generally plant material will not be needed at the back. Have all the foliage well-conditioned and cut into short sprigs, and the flowers on 8 cm

(3 in) stems in bowls of water to keep them really fresh until used.

4 · As with the swag, start by covering three sides of the whole garland with short sprigs of foliage, keeping the width constant. Distribute the different foliages equally along the length.

5 · When the mechanics are almost covered, start putting in the flowers, again mixing them along the full length so that although the groupings will vary, it will look well-spaced and colour-balanced. Mist spray the garland generously.

6 · Finally, fix the finished garland in position.

Checking the Arrangement

This garland was taken out to a garden statue and the wires joined across the back. Gentle shaping put the curves in the right place. As it was standing near a wall, the back was not likely to be seen, but the wires could have been covered with a twist of ivy if necessary. Almost invisible nylon fishing line can be used indoors as explained for the swag (see page 78).

Other Options

There are various other types of mechanics for a garland, depending on whether or not a water supply is needed.

Commercially made 'sausages' of foam are available in plastic cages, which hook together to make the desired length; or in shallow troughs, which fix together in a similar way.

The age-old method of tying or wiring bunches of foliage to overlap each other along a rope is still very practical, but an even cheaper and more effective way is to use nylon stockings or cut-off tights filled with soaked

sphagnum moss. As the nylons stretch almost indefinitely, you need to knot in a string of the required length to keep the measurement correct. The damp moss maintains a moist atmosphere around the garland to keep it fresh.

An all-foliage garland can be made a week before it is needed, laid in a shady spot in the garden and watered daily from a watering can with a fine rose on it. If flowers need to last in this type of garland, it is possible to make a number of holes in the nylon with a skewer to insert the stems into the soaked (but wrung-out) moss.

TOPIARY TREES

In recent years so-called 'topiary' trees have become very popular, especially when made in pairs to flank a doorway or entrance, as at the church porch for a wedding. They have also been used effectively to mark out paths across courtyards and gardens. Essentially easy to do after the mechanics have been mastered, they take a surprising amount of greenery, but flowers and fruit can be added in varying quantities.

OVERALL SIZE (W × H)
40 × 140 cm (16 × 54 in)

YOU WILL NEED
2 hazel poles or similar rustic poles 120 cm (48 in) long

2 flower pots 25 cm (10 in) in diameter

Pieces of broken brick or stone

10 kg (22 lb) bag ready-mix cement and sand

MECHANICS
2 green floral foam spheres 20 cm (8 in) in diameter

Thin polythene sheeting/cling film to cover foam

2 pieces 2.5 cm (1 in) wire mesh each 40 × 40 cm (16 × 16 in)

Reel wire, stout string

Kebab sticks, stub wires

PLANT MATERIAL
10–12 cm (4–5 in) lengths bay, box, choisya, pittosporum, skimmia, etc as available

Moss

10 stems spray chrysanthemums

10 spray carnations

10 alstroemeria

20 apricots

ACCESSORIES
9 m (10 yd) florist's waterproof ribbon, 5 cm (2 in) wide, in toning colour(s)

ARRANGER
Beverley Summers

1 · Hammer two nails, at right angles to each other, through each pole, one 10 cm (4 in) and the other 12 cm (4½ in) from the top. Using broken bricks or stones, wedge the poles in the flower pots so they are standing roughly upright.

2 · Mix the cement according to the manufacturer's instructions and work it into the flower pots between the stones, filling about three-quarters of each pot. Check from all sides, with a spirit level or plumb-bob, that the trunks are vertical. If possible tie them to a horizontal bar or chair back, check again, and leave them to set.

3 · Soak the foam balls, and cover first with polythene sheeting/ cling film and then with pieces of wire mesh. The polythene will help to conserve moisture, and the mesh will prevent the foam from breaking up. Leave them open at one end.

4 · When the trunks are set, impale the balls on them. The nails will prevent the balls from slipping down too far and provide a place to secure the covering wire mesh with string and/or reel wire. Even though none of this will show when the trees are finished, finish it off as neatly as possible, cutting away any excess wire mesh.

5 · The balls are now ready for decorating with greenery; the picture shows one half-completed. Strip the foliage of the lower leaves for about 5 cm (2 in).

6 · Cover the whole ball and if necessary clip it with scissors or shears to maintain a good sphere. Mix the various foliages evenly as you work.

7 · Arrange moss over the surface of the cement to cover it.

8 · Cut the flower stems into similar short lengths and again try to distribute the different flowers evenly. Add the apricots by impaling them on kebab sticks cut a little longer than the flower stalks. Used this way (rather than being wired), the fruit can be cooked or eaten afterwards.

9 · Twist stub wires around the ends of 1 m (3 ft) lengths of ribbon and push the wires up into the ball, or, for greater security in a breeze, twist the wires around the nails or wire mesh. Adjust the ribbon lengths so that they are not all equal, cutting across diagonally to taper the ends.

Checking the Arrangement

● The size of the trees can vary, from about 15 cm (6 in) high for table decorations (one for each guest to take home is always appreciated) to taller ones for large displays.
● The important thing is to keep good proportions between the head, the diameter of the trunk and the container. The head, soaked in water for fresh foliage and flowers, is always heavy and the cement and containers hould be weighty enough for stability, and also large enough to look right.
● The plant materials, too, need to be in proportion to the tree size. Small-leaved evergreens such as box, hebe and the finer cupressus are best for small trees. For small trees in small pots, plaster of Paris is a good medium to set the trunk in, as it dries out so quickly that the stick can be hand-held in its vertical position until the plaster has set.

Other Options

Although evergreens offer the most practical and naturalistic basis for topiary trees, *any* foliage can be used. Fantasy trees can be

made of, for example, statice, moss, honesty (lunaria) 'pennies', cut stalks, poppy seedheads, love-in-the-mist (nigella) seed-heads, fir cones, artificial leaf sprays and fruits.

Trees need not be circular either. Conical shapes look good, as does a tree made from a round and a cone on one trunk, or from three spheres in graded sizes with the smallest at the top.

A WELCOMING WREATH

We are now familiar with the welcoming front door wreath at Christmas, but it is much less usual at other times of the year. The wreath, as a circular garland of flowers and leaves, has for centuries played a part in joyful celebrations, standing for eternity, renewal and rebirth. What better way to greet friends and guests who come for drinks, for a party or to celebrate a wedding?

OVERALL SIZE
60 cm (24 in) in diameter

YOU WILL NEED
Circular ring of twigs or vines (bought or made – see step 1)
2 sardine tins
Gold spray paint

MECHANICS
2 small blocks soaked floral foam
Green sticky tape
Stub wire for hanging loop
Fine nylon fishing line (optional)

PLANT MATERIAL
A few twigs of contorted hazel or willow
Short pieces of cupressus
Trails of Rubus tricolor (or ivy)
5 stems alchemilla
10 yellow freesias
8 yellow roses

ARRANGER
Margaret Webster

1 · The wreath can be purchased, but it is easy to make your own if you can get a quantity of vine, wistaria or willow stems. Start by making a single strand into a rough circle the size you need. Fresh-cut stems are the easiest to handle; older, drier ones should be soaked in water first to make them pliable. Add other lengths of stem, intertwining them loosely with the first until you have the thickness you need. The wreath in the picture has then been bound over with a single strand, but this is not essential if the ends of the stems have been tucked in securely.

2 · Tuck strands and curls of contorted willow or hazel into the ring to give a slightly windswept and casual look.

3 · Tape the two tins, with their blocks of soaked foam, into the wreath in the 4 o'clock and 11 o'clock positions. The lower one goes on the inside of the circle, the top one on the outside.

4 · Now spray the whole thing *lightly* gold to give a festive gleam. Leave to dry.

5 · Make a wire loop for hanging and secure it to the back of the wreath. On the wreath in the photo a length of nylon fishing line was attached to the loop and taken up over the door to tie to a hinge and handle inside. The line is virtually invisible.

6 · Working *in situ*, so that the wreath is seen at the correct angle, cover the tins and foam with short pieces of cupressus (if you can get a blue-grey one it makes a good contrast with the yellow flowers) and arrange three or four rubus (or ivy) sprays to follow the curve. Introduce one or two sprays of lime-green alchemilla.

7 · Add four stems of freesia at the top and four at the bottom. Make good use of any curving stems to follow the circular line.

8 · Three roses in the top placement and five in the lower complete the ring. Tuck in one or two pieces of alchemilla or leaves if the mechanics show, but don't overcrowd it.

Checking the Arrangement

● This very effective decoration does not take long to do once the base ring is ready, and this can be prepared weeks in advance, leaving only the flowers and leaves to be arranged on the day.
● With the water supply in the foam-filled tins, the wreath will last up to a week, especially if given a misting spray of water whenever possible.

Other Options

A wreath like this can be used in many other places, such as on inside doors, over the fireplace or bedhead or complementing a mirror. There is another fine example on page 159.

The variations in decorating are as unlimited as your imagination. Fresh plant material can be used in all seasons: daffodils, forsythia and mimosa go well together in spring; colourful mixed flowers in summer; berries and fruits with autumn foliage; and evergreens with holly berries and cones at Christmas.

Dried materials, of course, are equally suitable, and the range of dried and preserved seedheads, leaves and made-up flowers offers enormous scope. Artificial flowers and fruits are other possibilities.

Chapter five · Review

*A*lthough wreaths, garlands and swags are age-old decorations, created 'topiary' trees are a comparatively recent development of the flower arranger's art. All are especially useful for festivals in churches and stately homes because they can often emulate or draw attention to similar designs in tapestries, architectural decorations, carvings, tombs, stained glass and plasterwork.

Practial Aspects

The availability of floral foams has made the mechanics easier to set up, but many arrangers nevertheless prefer to use moss as the basis for any of these decorations.

Making a garland can be a communal or team effort because the actual arranging is fairly repetitive once the design, colour scheme and mechanics have been settled. Flowers and foliage are generally then provided by one organizer who allocates the work to be done.

Glue guns

Electric glue guns, which utilize hot glue, have not been mentioned so far in the chapter, but they do speed up quite a lot of the work when dried, preserved or artificial materials are being used. Because the glue cools and sets so rapidly, cones, shells, fruits, etc, are fixed in seconds, when with tube glues you would need to hold them in place for minutes. Handle the gun with great care because it is easy to burn fingers both on the hot glue and the tip of the gun. *Never, never* leave the gun plugged in when not in use or where young children can reach it.

Variations on the theme

Topiary trees, wreaths, garlands and swags offer enormous scope for improvisation. Here are some ideas; either copy them exactly, or use them as inspiration for creations of your own.

TREES

All the following suggestions are based on a trunk set in cement/plaster of Paris in a flower pot with an outer cover.

(1) A tree built on a cone of soaked foam, with box or cupressus, closely clipped and banded diagonally with artificial Christmas roses or small fruits.

(2) Dried and artificial fruits in a formal cone painted in either terracotta, gold or white and then 'antiqued' with grey, black or green paint to look like verdigris.

(3) A trunk of twisted vine or other gnarled branch with reindeer moss pinned, and statice pushed, into a ball made of 2.5 cm (1 in) wire mesh packed with dry foam.

(4) Clipped mixed evergreens in three spheres of foam on one straight trunk. Arrange the three spheres first and then shear each of them all over to emulate garden topiary.

(5) A green moss-covered ball of foam with branched trunk. Spray regularly to keep moss moist and green. Use cupressus or other evergreen foliage at the base.

(6) Hoops of thick basketry cane fixed on a central pole and decorated with ribbon bows and ivy trails, to make a modern variation of the centuries-old Kissing Bough.

(7) Similar to No. 4, but instead of three spheres use a cone and a ball in clipped evergreens, standing in a basket.

(8) A tree of foil crepe-paper leaves wired on to a central trunk of thick wire, with artificial fruits or baubles hanging from the branches. It can also be made from plastic leaves taken off a Christmas spray, wired and re-assembled. Cover the base cement with moss, gravel, bark, cones, broken windscreen glass or foliage to suit the style.

WREATHS AND GARLANDS

(9) Holly and artificial berry clusters made on a mossed wreath ring, with large scarlet bow of waterproof ribbon.

(10) For a table centrepiece, a polystyrene ring covered in reindeer moss, cross-gartered with ribbon, with a small piece of cling-film-wrapped foam taped on to hold a few fresh flowers and foliage.

(11) An oval twined vine decorated with small artificial grapes and leaves.

(12) A straw wreath, decorated with crinkled paper ribbon, a Hallowe'en mask or cut-out gourd, and ivy.

(13) A twig wreath with two birds, a nest and spring flowers.

(14) A table centre in a foam-packed, ring-shaped plastic trough, with fresh foliage, flowers and matching candles.

(15) A garland of fresh flowers and leaves, similar to the garland on page 80, for either a tall column or a church pillar.

SWAGS

(**16**) Gates swagged in evergreens and decorated with flat-backed circular swags of fresh flowers and leaves.

(**17**) Hanging from a wooden ring a two-swag version on a single rope, bar or ribbon. The shapes can vary to suit the position.

(**18**) Autumn leaves, cones and berries in floral foam which has been covered with cling film and then strapped on to a wood batten.

(**19**) A three-section swag on cord or ribbon in fresh or dried materials.

(**20**) A very dainty swag, in the style of Robert Adam, painted in matt white to simulate carved plasterwork.

(**21**) A wall trophy in Grinling Gibbons style in high relief, looking like carved natural wood.

(**22**) A Roman-style *encarpa*, which is a horizontal festoon of flowers and fruits, as seen in paintings and in sculpture.

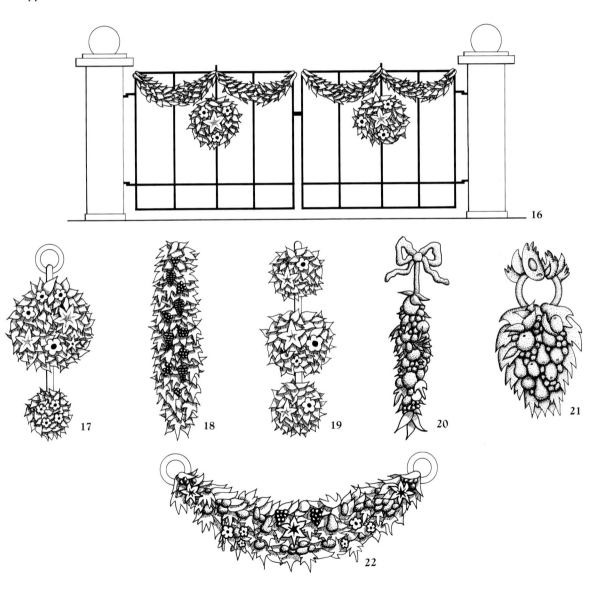

Chapter Six

FREESTYLES AND ABSTRACTS

The so-called 'modern' styles – freestyle and abstract – developed after the 1950s, influenced by Japanese flower arranging (ikebana) and by general design trends. Painting, sculpture, architecture, furniture and ceramics were developing simple, uncluttered lines; forms were geometric or inspired by nature, and textural interest began to be derived from materials themselves rather than from applied decoration. In modern flower arrangements much less plant material is used than in traditional massed arrangements, and space is a positive element in itself.

*T*raditional styles of arranging in Britain and the West have always been massed with flowers and leaves in profusion and stems generally radiating from a point in the centre of the container. More often than not, balance has been symmetrical, and outlines principally triangular.

Japanese arranging (ikebana), on the other hand, is always asymmetrical and uses carefully selected and limited amounts of plant material, with space an important design factor. The influence of ikebana on Western arranging began to be felt in the 1950s, along with the other trends towards modernity which prevailed in all aspects of design.

The Emergence of Freestyle

With these influences all around it was unlikely that flower arrangement could remain unaffected. Simplified arrangements began to appear using far fewer materials and often only two or three different types, as in the picture on page 93. Since the cluttered look was out and plain walls and streamlined furniture were in, there was space to show off simpler outlines and bold shapes. These designs were then described as 'modern' or 'contemporary'. The epithet 'modern' still continues (in much the same way as it is used in the term 'modern art'), though 'freestyle' is now the more accurate and internationally accepted description.

Generally, stems still radiated from a central point, though containers with one or more openings became popular as they offered more variation from the traditional approach.

For the most part, plant material was used naturistically in the way that it grew, but arrangers began to experiment with looping and knotting pliable stems, (vines and willows), clipping and reshaping leaves (iris, palm fans, tulip, bergenia) and de-foliating stems (lime, roses, old man's beard, ivy) to give cleaner, more defined lines. Non-plant materials were introduced, including plastic piping, nylon rope, shells, industrial waste and *objets trouvés* from the beach, the rubbish dump or the salvage yard.

The Development of Abstract Designs

Inevitably this led flower arrangers to look enquiringly at the potential *design* features of plant materials available to them, not just as horticultural specimens attractive in themselves, but as units of colour, line, shape or texture.

Because an open rose was a colourful, velvety, circular form it could be used as just that in a pattern of plant material which paid absolutely no regard to the way the rose grew in the garden.

Similarly, a delphinium was a blue cylinder, an apple a red sphere and an arum leaf a glossy, green triangle. This was a very big step for true gardeners and plantsmen/women to take and many did not like it at all. But to the arrangers who at heart had been designers first and foremost, it offered enormous scope and freedom to create arrangements in any way they chose.

Plant Material

As freestyle and abstract arranging developed, it soon became apparent that the mechanics and, where needed, a water supply were going to be the two principal problems. This explains why dried and preserved plant materials are so often used in these two forms of arranging – they are light and not difficult to support, and they need no water. They do lack colour, however, and this has given rise to a good deal of painting of dried stems, leaves and seedheads.

Plant material for freestyles and abstracts is chosen for its bold shape, strong line or interesting texture, rather than for prettiness. Hogweed stems and seedheads, alliums, coconut spathes, cones, blade leaves and strong round flowers such as chrysanthemums, dahlias, gerberas and open roses are much used, as well as exotic strelitzias and anthuriums. But there are no limits and no restrictions, and if a bunch of primroses or a cluster of cypress meets the needs of the design, that's fine.

Containers, Mechanics and Water Supply

In traditional work the container is chosen to suit the flower arrangement, but it remains a feature of the display in its own right. In abstract work the container should be an integral part of the design and not obviously a container.

Because the plant material is limited, there is little to hide either container or mechanics, so they have to be contrived with care and for each design. For abstract work containers and mechanics may be needed at several points in the design and quite often one point can be on a background, especially in show-work. Stems are taken through a hole to a phial of water fixed behind. Others may be needed in driftwood, behind spathes or in a hollow stem. Orchid tubes are usually large enough for one or two stems, or cigar tubes can be cut to the desired length and glued or wired in place. If they cannot be hidden they should be painted to tone in with their support, or perhaps have a matching piece of stem, wood or spathe glued over to conceal them.

For the largest part of the design a pinholder may be easier to hide than floral foam.

SIMPLE FREESTYLE

This delicate freestyle arrangement is typical of many that have been popular since the early 1960s. Plant material is strictly limited and confined to three different types, each having a very different shape and texture. Space is of prime importance. It is featured not only in the actual arrangement, but within the plant material itself in the cane loops, in the container, in the accessories and even in the oriental table on which the arrangement stands.

OVERALL SIZE (W × H)
40 × 90 cm (16 × 36 in)

YOU WILL NEED
Container with simple lines, like this round bowl raised on a conical base

MECHANICS
Lead pinholder 7 cm (3 in) in diameter
Putty-type adhesive

PLANT MATERIAL
2 m (2¼ yd) thick basketry cane
3 bergenia leaves
2 longiflorum lilies

ACCESSORIES
2–3 white pebbles with holes

ARRANGER
Sheila Gordon

1 · Cut the basketry cane into three lengths: 90 cm (36 in), 60 cm (24 in) and 50 cm (20 in). Soak thoroughly until pliable, then loop and knot one end of the longest piece and one of the others. Tie with string or wire if necessary to hold the loops. The third length should be left unknotted but twisted into a loose coil, and tied with string. Leave all three to dry thoroughly before cutting any ties.

2 · Fix the pinholder with putty-type adhesive to the centre of the container bowl. The tallest cane should be at least two and a half times the height of the container and impaled on the pinholder towards the back. It helps to make a cross-cut at the bottom of the stem first. This first placement is important: the loops at the top should be vertically over the point where the cane is held on the pinholder. This will give good balance and prevent it appearing to tip over.

3 · The second stem is much shorter (two-thirds the length of the main stem) and fixed to the *left* of the first. The downward curving stem will be twisted all the way along (if too tight pull the cane gently to open out) and fixed on the right. Adjust the length so it clears the table.

4 · Arrange the bergenia leaves next: two to the left with the front one curving over the container rim, and a slightly longer-stemmed one on the right following the line of the lowest piece of cane.

5 · The two lilies are placed last. The one to the left and back should have a slightly longer stem; the shorter one looks up towards the viewer.

Checking the Arrangement

● As there are so few items to arrange, it is obviously important that each be well-placed and with just the right length of stem and angle in relation to the others.
● With much more space within the arrangement than has been used so far in the book, the voids are as important as the solid forms. The spaces may be completely enclosed as in the tied cane loops, or only partly defined as in the gaps between the cane stems and between the leaves, and even in the trumpet shapes of the lilies.
● If you can look at the arrangement against a plain background and try to visualize the open spaces as solids – a sort of negative photograph of the finished display – you will appreciate how space can be used to full advantage and as a positive design factor. A photograph can only show you a two-dimensional picture, and all flower arrangements are three-dimensional. In this one there is almost as much depth from front to back as there is width from side to side.
● All the other ingredients of this design also have space within them (holes in the pebbles and in the triangular space dividing the conical base of the container). It stands on a table with carved open decoration and within a space defined by an arched alcove.

Other Options

Curving vines (clematis, wistaria), willow stems or fasciated willow can take the place of cane, and any bold leaves such as arum, hosta, rhododendron or laurel can be used. Flowers too need to be bold; try anthuriums, large chrysanthemums and dahlias, or clusters of smaller flowers grouped to look like one or two large ones. Emphasize boldness and clarity.

INSPIRED BY DRIFTWOOD

Every flower arranger, it seems, longs to possess a really fine piece of driftwood and is prepared to walk miles along beaches, by river-banks or through woods in the hope of finding it. Such sorties are often rewarded, but this marvellous piece was bought from a sales table at a NAFAS show. As a decorative sculptural piece it needs nothing added, yet it can be an inspiration for a landscape scene or a freestyle design as in the picture. Alternatively, it can be part of a larger interpretative exhibit as seen on pages 127 and 129.

OVERALL SIZE (W × H)
40 × 92 cm (16 × 36 in)

YOU WILL NEED
Small dish

MECHANICS
Piece of soaked floral foam
Lead-based metal foam holder
Kebab sticks
Putty-type adhesive

PLANT MATERIAL
Large piece of driftwood
5 oranges
10 vine leaves (Vitis coignetiae)

ARRANGER
Molly Watson

Driftwood that is bought will already have had the rotten bits cleaned away, been treated for woodworm and probably been mounted, as this piece was, on a small plywood or chipboard base. If you find your own piece, however, you will have work to do, but it will assuredly be worth the effort.

1 · If you have found, rather than bought, the driftwood, it will need to be prepared. Wood found on a lake or sea-shore or out on the moors will probably have been dried out by the sun and wind and have a grey sheen; if so clean it gently, to preserve the grey colour. Other wood may need scrubbing thoroughly with water, detergent and disinfectant to remove dirt and insects; allow it to dry out slowly in the sun, or any warm, dry place. Remove any areas of soft, rotting wood with an old knife, leaving only the hard wood, which must then be brushed with a wire brush.

2 · Now is the time to consider the shape and how well the piece stands. Look at it from all angles before deciding to remove anything. If a branching bit needs to be sawn off, save the piece as it may come in handy as a support.

3 · Stand the driftwood in position, seeking the most pleasing profile in its setting.

4 · Place the dish with the soaked foam at the front. The foam is held on a lead-based foam holder with metal prongs because extra weight will be needed to support the oranges.

5 · Impale three oranges on a kebab stick (or on two if one is not long enough) and two on another stick. The three oranges go into the foam. If there is no convenient ledge for the top oranges it may be necessary to drill a small hole in the driftwood to take the end of the stick. The hole can be filled later if necessary, but it may always be useful and need not show. The smooth roundness of the oranges is a complete contrast with the rough wood.

6 · The flame-coloured leaves are the autumn glory of the decorative vine (*Vitis coignetiae*), the finest of all ornamental vines, which looks splendid growing over an arch or pergola. They are layered in continental fashion towards the front and side, with a spray trailing out over the stonework.

Checking the Arrangement

● The piles of oranges must be vertical to counteract the slant of the wood.
● When using driftwood it is often tempting to use its spaces for groupings of other plant material because there is convenient ledge for a container. But the enclosed and partly enclosed voids are an important part of the design and should not be filled. The two groups of oranges here have been thoughtfully placed with the solid spheres echoing the rounded open spaces. Check that your spaces have been well used.

Other Options

A large piece of driftwood can be finished in a number of ways. It can be made to stand with one or two 'legs', which are pieces that either have been sawn off, or are from other wood or dowelling. Alternatively, the bottom can be levelled if it is well-balanced. Or, if it is a small piece, it can be permanently set in a base of plaster, which will later be hidden by plant material. Other alternatives include screwing it permanently to a wooden base,

inserting a purchased lead base with a screw; or using a purchased driftwood clamp, which incorporates an inverted pinholder to fit into another pinholder.

After cleaning and cutting to shape, driftwood can be wax polished, varnished, bleached, painted, sprayed or touched up with shoe polish, but unless it is for something special most people like to keep it in as natural a state as possible as it is more versatile that way.

The NAFAS Handbook of Schedule Definitions describes driftwood as 'any bark, branch, wood or root in a dry condition excluding seedpods and spathes'. Small pieces of wood are very useful for obscuring small containers and for adding to landscape designs. Try to collect a few to add to your collection of useful items.

Another useful source of interesting wood is ivy (hedera). Stripped of its hairy bark down to the smooth, hard heart-wood, it dries to a pale biscuit colour. If cut while still growing, the outer bark will strip away easily with a sharp knife, though it can be a long job. If the ivy has dried, soak the piece in water for several days before tackling the stripping. Sturdy pieces can be made to stand by adding blocks or peg-legs. Slender pieces can add pleasing lines to freestyle designs, and sturdier, tangled pieces can be used to make a stand, as on page 129.

Driftwood can often be arranged with just two or three bold flowers to make a pleasing decoration. The roughness of the wood contrasts well with the velvety smoothness of roses or amaryllis or the silkiness of lilies.

Bold leaves such as fatsia, bergenia, arum, hosta or mahonia also go well with it.

Never be content to use a piece of driftwood in just one way. Lay it on its side and turn it upside-down, considering all the possibilities.

STRAIGHT AND CURVED

Freestyle arrangements need not always be so economical of material, but the impact of an unusual outline is still important, and spaces and solids still need to be strongly contrasted. This arrangement uses both dried and fresh materials and demonstrates clearly the value of contrasts: straight leaves with curving lines, round flowers with tufted ones. Even the rounded pot stands on triangular bases. None of the other freestyle designs in this chapter, as it happens, uses painted plant material, but here the effectiveness of black is fully shown.

OVERALL SIZE (W × H)
60 × 106 cm (24 × 42 in)

YOU WILL NEED
Black paint or spray
Bowl or basin painted black
2 black triangular bases (perspex or painted hardboard)

MECHANICS
Block of soaked floral foam
Large foam anchor
Putty-type adhesive

PLANT MATERIAL
3 stems fasciated willow
3 long stems New Zealand flax
6 pink gerberas
3 heads eucomis

ARRANGER
Marian Aaronson

1 · Fix the foam anchor to the bottom of the bowl with putty-type adhesive and cut the soaked foam block to fit, but only to come about halfway up the bowl. It will not be visible when the arrangement is complete.

2 · Paint or spray black the willow stems. Use them to make a three-dimensional curving outline with plenty of space in the centre.

3 · Decide on the final height, bearing in mind the length of the black stems in proportion to the bowl and the bases. Cut one flax leaf either taller or shorter than the tallest curve. Place it centrally, towards the back of the container. A second leaf goes in front of the first. The third is cut shorter still and placed to the right and a little behind the others.

4 · The cut-off pieces of flax are used to make another placement of leaves on the side nearest to the shortest black curve. Be sure the leaves are cut and placed at a pleasing angle, with the longest sides toward the centre.

5 · The gerberas are put in next and should, as far as possible, face in different directions to avoid an all-facing-the-front, flat look. The tallest follows the line of the side leaves and the stem is placed between them, with the flower head tilting upwards and inwards, strengthening the in-curving lines of the willow.

6 · Four other gerberas follow a roughly diagonal line downwards and to the left, then the sixth flower curves forward over the container rim.

7 · Finally, three heads of eucomis, cut quite short, are inserted at the back, at the bottom of the tallest curving stem. They give the necessary depth and some appearance of weight behind the stems. Their line counterbalances that of the cut flax leaves.

Checking the Arrangement

● This open-plan arrangement makes a bold display piece against a fairly plain wall, especially if the light comes from one side to emphasize the modelling of the flower petals and to cast interesting shadows. It will also highlight the difference between the flat-faced gerberas and the rounded, textured and tufted eucomis.

● The arrangement shows the value of using complementary colours (see also page 000) for impact. Red and green are the complementaries chosen here – pink being a tint of red. Black, generally called neutral or 'achromatic', provides a foil.

● It is always a good design feature to repeat the colouring of the container within the plant material. A white bowl might have called for the outlines to be white rather than black, and then the whole mood of the arrangement would be changed and the whole colour scheme need to be rethought.

Other Options

The general outline and composition could be adapted in any number of ways.

The open outline could be established with vines, basketry cane, stripped ivy, burnt gorse from heathland or tree branches cut and trimmed to give a curving shape. The strong vertical could be iris or yucca leaves or, perhaps more interestingly, small bundles of stalks or sticks. Alternative flowers should be bold and round in shape, such as roses, dahlias, peonies or single-bloom chrysanthemums. You could also consider using fruit with oranges or lemons perhaps, mounted on kebab sticks. It would be interesting to try lilies – either arums or longiflorums – but once the main flowers are changed all kinds of adjustments might need to be made.

That is the endless fascination of freestyle designing. While the finished product may only employ a limited number of pieces of plant material, the trying-out and 'playing around' beforehand will require all kinds of things to be considered. This will mean that the arranger has to look very thoroughly at the design possibilities and the inter-relationships of plant materials.

FORM, TEXTURE AND SPACE

When no flowers at all are used in a strongly sculptural design, many people query whether it really comes under the heading of 'flower arrangement'. But who, other than a flower arranger, would construct a piece of sculpture from palm sheaths and moss? The inspiration for this arrangement came from the colours of the abstract painting by Carl Brisson with its textured pattern of squares and circles in grey, brown and a pinkish-tan. The colours suggested dried and preserved materials at once, and as soon as the design process got under way, flowers never really looked like the answer.

OVERALL SIZE (W × H)
45 × 106 cm (18 × 42 in)

YOU WILL NEED
Large hand-thrown pottery container
Piece of slate or stone

MECHANICS
2 short pieces bamboo cane
Glue, strong sticky tape
Stub wires and reel wire
Pieces of dry foam (brown)

PLANT MATERIAL
2 large palm sheaths
Reindeer moss

ARRANGER
Iris Moss

It is unlikely that you will find a container quite like this, but a heavy pot with a wide top opening, standing about 30 cm (13 in) high and preferably in earthy colouring, will serve very well. This design is all about composing with what is available. There should be no preconceived composition, just a feeling, at this early stage, of 'seeing what can be done with the palm sheaths' to create an interesting three-dimensional display.

1 · Set the container on the slate or stone base at a slightly diagonal angle to accentuate depth. With so little plant material being used, the result can easily be rather flat, so you should make the most of every opportunity to add to the illusion of depth. Wedge pieces of dry-foam into the container to fill about one half to two-thirds.

2 · Cut two pieces of bamboo cane, each about 10 cm (4 in) long, and split each one in half vertically. Wrap the bottom end of each palm sheath and two of the pieces of bamboo together to make a double leg or stem. Use glue or wire to secure them, and tape over neatly to make it firm.

3 · When the 'legs' are set, take the shorter piece of palm and place it in the right-hand side of the container at a slight angle from the absolute vertical. Now take the second piece and 'offer' it from the left-hand side, testing where the bend should be put in a happy relationship with the first sheath. Before you crease the bend firmly, consider if one or both pieces need trimming.

4 · The design could be left at this point if a satisfying shape with a pleasing *space* has been achieved,

but more interest can be added with some contrasting forms. The arranger felt that the strength of the design called for something unusual, so 'flowers' were made from reindeer moss. Small pieces of moss were bunched together, and bound with reel wire. Three of the five bunches have a short stub wire 'stem' and are put at the container rim on the left. The top bunch is wired in place through the palm and the bottom one simply lies on the base.

Checking the Arrangement

● The container here is an unusual one and its split shape, as well as the colour, undoubtedly influenced the arranger's choice of outline material. The whole design is large and weighty, despite the limited amount of plant material. In the large modern room in which it was photographed it drew the eye towards the picture that had inspired it.
● The point at which you arrange the palm sheaths is the true designing stage; the whole sculpture will stand or fall (literally probably, as well as figuratively) on how the two palm sheaths are brought together. They may actually meet and touch, or there may need to be a space, as here. No two sheaths are identical and the arranger has to visualize the proportions before cutting.

Other Options

Abstract arrangements can never truly be copied, but they can give inspiration for something similar. There are not many plant materials that give such a bold outline, but driftwood, stripped ivy, coconut spathes or dried kelp could achieve a similar shape.

Fresh flowers could be used very effectively (especially in a bright colour) as long as they were bold in form, such as hippeastrum,

anthurium, dahlia or poinsettia. The choice of pot will certainly influence the choice of flowers.

Fresh flowers would require a water supply in three places: an orchid tube of wet foam probably glued to the left-hand palm sheath, and one lying on the base hidden perhaps by the flower(s); then a larger tube or piece of wet foam in a small tin could be pushed into the vase on top of the dry foam, to accommodate two or three stems there.

In a setting with some green in it, bold foliage could equally well be used. Fruit is a possibility too (as on page 125), but in this case the top placement would probably have to be abandoned because of weight.

PURE ABSTRACTION

Abstract arrangements like any other style can be purely decorative, with no meaning at all, or they can have a title and tell a story or portray an occasion or mood. This design was simply an interesting study in curves and asymmetrical balance, yet it could well be given a title suggesting that it is something more: 'Skate-boarding' and 'The Seventh Wave' (the big one for surfers) have both been suggested. At this stage of arranging there should be no wish or need to copy what another arranger has done, but it is still interesting to analyse how the design has been put together.

OVERALL SIZE (W × H)
90 × 90 cm (35 × 35 in)

COMPONENTS
Earth-brown round pot
Smaller circular unglazed pot

MECHANICS
Soaked floral foam in taller pot
Putty-type adhesive

PLANT MATERIAL
2 curled palm spathes
Piece of skeletonized opuntia (prickly pear)
Glycerined fatsia leaf, trimmed into a circular shape
Piece of wood with wavy edge
Ball-like seedhead
5 red anthuriums

ARRANGER
Marian Aaronson

The remarkable feature about abstract work in any medium is that the viewer puts his own interpretation on what he sees and this is often far removed from what the artist thought of or intended. With abstract work, that does not matter. What matters is that the artist has made the viewer think and react.

1 · The tallest palm spathe is fixed in the taller back pot, the curl facing backwards but at a slight angle.

2 · A piece of skeletonized opuntia and the fatsia leaf are fixed with putty-type adhesive to the back of the straight part of the spathe to add interest.

3 · The piece of wood with a wavy edge is supported horizontally from the back pot.

4 · The smaller pot is placed to the front and half to the left of the other container. The second spathe rests on this, with the curl over the pot and the 'stem' pointing to the right and back. A little putty-type adhesive secures it.

5 · The ball-like seedhead rests inside the curls and is fixed with a little putty-type adhesive. Its mottled colouring links the light and dark containers.

6 · The anthuriums have their stems in the soaked foam of the back pot and are arranged to bring the heads into a horizontal line above the front spathe and following its line.

Checking the Arrangement

● In abstract arranging the containers are an integral part of the design. Here, although the back container actually holds the main part of the design and water-retaining foam for the fresh anthuriums, the front one is merely a support. But they are both rounded like the palm curls, and the clever use of the ball-shaped seedhead echoes the pot shapes and makes a pattern of the three and a repetition of the curves. Sometimes this sort of combination is a happy accident, but more often than not the arranger has actively sought a way of creating this effect. Any sort of repetition gives rhythm to the design and carries the eye through it.

● Few homes will have the kind of décor to provide a setting for abstract arrangements like this one. They are mostly for shows, to demonstrate the ingenuity of the arranger. A class of some 15 or more exhibits, all interpreting, say, 'Fire of Anguish' (as at the NAFAS Competitions at Brighton in 1989), can fascinate the general public as well as fellow flower arrangers. They will seek to understand each exhibit and, in seeking, will use their own experience, background, general knowledge and emotions to work out an explanation.

Other Options

Abstract designs are not really copyable, so, as an exercise, try to design a modern/abstract exhibit to interpret one or more of the following titles, which have appeared in recent show schedules: 'Cavorting in Space', 'Vibrant Variations', 'Iridescence', 'Redevelopment', 'Spellbound', 'The Form Emerges', 'Sequence', 'Eye of the Wind', 'Chiaroscuro', 'Impressionism', 'The Nuclear Age', 'Calligraphy', 'Ever-whirling Wheels of Change'.

CHAPTER SIX · REVIEW

*T*he first 'modern' styles, more accurately called freestyle arranging, were influenced by modern design trends in the West and also by ikebana from the East. Abstract was a development from the first simplified freestyle arrangements and is a more complex discipline. Many consider it unsuited to a craft that uses a naturalistic medium like plant material; others find it stimulating and creative.

Characteristics of Freestyles

● Plant materials are still used in a more or less naturalistic way, though there may be some trimming, looping and manipulating.
● Flowers, foliage and seedheads are chosen for their bold shapes, strong lines or interesting textures.
● Plant materials are limited in number and type.
● Space is a very important feature of the design.
● Containers have a simplified, often geometric form with textural interest. Two or more openings offer a change from the traditional.
● Balance is more likely to be asymmetrical than symmetrical.
● Because so little plant material is used, contrast of colour, size and shape is chosen for impact and there is virtually no transition.
● Proportions may be exaggerated: height or width, for example, may be two or three times that of the container.
● Bases, backgrounds and accessories, if used, are in keeping – tailored, textured, stylized.

Characteristics of Abstracts

Abstract designs take all these points a stage further, always moving farther away from traditional work. The verb 'to abstract' means to represent the essence, to strip away non-essentials, to summarize, and abstract flower arrangements use any possible means to show the essence of a pattern, an idea or a mood.

● Plant material is chosen for its design features and is rarely used naturalistically. It may be cut, bent, folded, painted, twisted, sliced and used however the design requires.
● The ingredients are pared down to essentials and all unnecessary items discarded.
● The container(s), if they can be seen, are an integral feature of the design, not just supports or holders of water. This means they usually have to be devised specifically for each exhibit.
● Accessories, if used, will either be abstracted in themselves (for example, a Henry Moore type figure) or be items of non-plant material selected for shape, texture or colour to enhance the plant material.
● In show or display work, where a base and/or backing can be used, these often provide support for some of the plant material and a water supply if needed; this helps to give greater depth.
● Instead of the central focus of interest found in most traditional designs, abstract designs may have a number of interest points distributed throughout.
● There is no limit to the way in which abstract arrangements may experiment with ideas and ways of using plant materials. Abstract is not so much a style as an exploration.

Plant Materials

While by no means exhaustive, the following lists include the types of plant material well suited to freestyle and abstract designs:

Stems: bamboo, basketry cane, hazel (corkscrew), ivy (stripped), hogweed, leycesteria, mitsumata, vines, willow (curly and fasciated)

Foliage: artichoke, arum, bergenia, begonia, broom, croton, cycas palm, fatshedera, fatsia, hosta, iris, ivy, mahonia, monstera, palm fan (chamerops), New Zealand flax (phormium), yucca

Flowers: achillea, agapanthus, amaryllis (hippeastrum), anthurium, carnation, chrysanthemum, clivia, dahlia, delphinium, eremurus, forsythia, gerbera, gladiolus, heleconia, hyacinth, hydrangea, liatris, lily, poinsettia, protea, rhododendron, rose, stock, strelitzia, tulip, willow (pussy)

Seedheads, etc: bulrush (reedmace), coconut spathes, Chinese lantern (physalis), pine cones, driftwood.

Containers

Abstract work requires containers that are integral to the design, and modern pottery is often suitable because of its textural finish (see page 101) or because of its shape (page 99). Sometimes, a container can be devised from some of the plant material used in the design, for example, spathes, hollow stems or fruit. Driftwood often has a hollow or curve that will conceal a small container.

Freestyle designing offers great scope for the imagination, but it also poses a problem for any arranger who has only traditional containers. Containers for freestyle designs need to have a 'modern' look. Baskets may provide an answer; their texture is always interesting and there is a vast range of shapes.

Look out for well-shaped plastic containers in the supermarkets. They can be cut quite easily with scissors and then painted, with some sand or grit mixed in for textural interest. Tall tins or plastic cylinders can be wound with sea-grass or string. Do-it-yourself stores and builders' merchants can yield interesting pipes and joints, building bricks and blocks. Reject shops often have cheap china or glass to paint or spray.

Interpretative Use

Freestyle and abstract designs can be purely decorative, to be enjoyed simply because they are pleasing to look at. Or, as happens more often in shows and exhibitions, they can be designed to tell a story, express a mood or even make some social comment. The flower arranger becomes an artist in the wider sense of using his/her medium of plant material to communicate a message to the onlooker.

Freestyle and abstract arrangements often provide a means of interpreting titles and themes. Because good interpretative work makes use of the plant materials' physical characteristics of colour, form, line and texture, and of its symbolic associations (for example, the poppy signifies sleep, the thistle evokes Scotland, and black is associated with evil), freestyles and abstracts will show these more clearly than a massed design. Their exciting lines, carefully chosen ingredients, asymmetry and new ideas are also more likely to attract the judge's eye!

Chapter Seven

DECORATING THE CHURCH

Being asked to help to 'do the church flowers' may be an arranger's first venture in floral decorating outside the home. Knowing what to expect and what is required goes a long way towards overcoming a natural diffidence, and sensible preparation will save time and frustration.
Whether your place of worship is a tiny country chapel or grand city church, a tabernacle or temple, there will be many features in common where flower arrangements are concerned. Above all, these decorations must not, at any time, interfere with the church ritual, impede the clergy, block the view of the congregation or choir or in any way hamper the conduct of services.

*C*hurch *flower arrangements* must be designed according to the wishes and customs of the church. They can perhaps be more innovative and interpretative for special festivals to give church members and visitors a change from what has always been done. Floor parallels, pot-et-fleur, dried and preserved materials, swags and garlands could all be suitable for these occasions.

The Flower Rota

If your name has now been put on the flower rota and this is your first time of arranging, be sure you know:
● the day and times when flowers can be done
● whether the church will be open, or where a key is kept
● if you must supply your own flowers and foliage; and if so, whether there is an allowance from a flower fund
● if any foliage may be cut from the churchyard or shrubberies
● where the arrangements are needed; if on the altar, what colour the frontal will be
● where to get water and dispose of rubbish
● what to do with the flowers from the previous week
● whether containers, mechanics, etc are provided at the church and where they are kept
● whether it is your responsibility to top-up and maintain the arrangements during the week, or whether someone else does this.
Nothing is more frustrating, especially if you live some distance away, than to arrive with your flowers and find that you cannot get in, or that there are no mechanics available, or that you don't know where there is a water supply. So until you know the ropes, prepare for every emergency.

Do not feel shy about asking these very basic questions, because if you are going to do a good job, you need to know the answers. Very few churches are sufficiently organized that they can provide a sheet telling you all this. Beware too, of the comment that 'there's plenty of foam in the flower cupboard' – this will probably turn out to be old, bone-dry and honeycombed with holes!

A checklist of what to take with you to the church is given on page 118.

Scale

There are two important differences in arranging in church, instead of at home, which need to be appreciated from the start: the difference in scale and the need to think carefully about colour.

Even the smallest chapel will be considerably bigger than the average room at home; the furnishings too will be larger and the light may well be dimmer. Flower arrangements will generally be viewed from a greater distance, except at the font or in a side chapel for private prayer.

Flowers and leaves therefore need to be fairly bold and simple in outline. The large mop-head chrysanthemums or cactus dahlias which would be far too big for most home arrangements will just suit a church window or altar. Small, fussy flowers will seldom be effective, but the stately spikes of gladioli or delphiniums, and the clear bold shapes of lilies, peonies, tulips and roses will show up well. Larger leaves like bergenia, hosta, fatsia and aspidistra can give strength and impact to a church arrangement.

Arrangers often think that much *more* plant material is needed but this is not so. What *is* needed is bolder and larger material with longer stems.

Colours

Many older churches are dark. Stained-glass windows reduce the light, while dark wood, heavy carvings and large tombs or statues create dark corners.

Even in modern, generally lighter, buildings it is the *luminous* colours that show up well. These are what we generally call pastel colourings: white, cream, lemon, pink, apricot, mauve and pale blue. To these you can add the so-called advancing colours of yellow, orange, lime green and bright orangey-red.

Any dark colour, especially the darkest greens, blues and purples, loses its identity in poor light and simply looks black from a distance. It may, however, be necessary sometimes to use dark foliage as a foil to the flowers and to help show them up, especially where there is a confused or patterned background behind the altar or on window sills, where the light comes from behind.

Traditional Requirements

The rest of this chapter shows how to tackle arrangements in the places where they are usually needed: on the altar, at the font, in windows, by the pulpit and on pew ends for special occasions. They are all fairly traditional, as that is what is generally expected in places of worship.

There are, of course, modern churches with simple interiors, clean-cut lines and space. If yours is one of them, look back at Chapter 6 and consider whether one of the ideas there might be adapted to complement some feature of the architecture or furnishings.

FLOWERS FOR THE ALTAR

Flowers on the altar, the most important in the church, are generally seen only from a distance by most of the congregation, so the sculptural trumpet shape of lilies makes them an ideal choice. Traditionally, the finest flowers are used on the altar, and throughout the ages lilies have been associated with the Madonna and have symbol-ized purity. It is important that altar flowers should not dominate the cross, but rather lead the eye towards it, making a balanced grouping with this central feature.

OVERALL SIZE (W×H)
60×50 cm (24×20 in) on each side of the cross

YOU WILL NEED
2 troughs or bread tins about 25 cm (10 in) long, painted a neutral stone colour

MECHANICS
*2 blocks of soaked floral foam
White sticky tape*

PLANT MATERIAL
*8 stems longiflorum lilies
Rhododendron leaf sprays
8 hosta leaves, lime-edged if possible
A few stems of sweet rocket (Hesperis matronalis)*

ARRANGER
Jennifer Le May

1 · Lay out a sheet of polythene to protect the altar cloth on either side of the cross, and have a cloth ready to mop up any spills quickly. Cut each block of foam to about two-thirds the length of the trough and a little narrower; it should protrude at least 4 cm (1½ in) above the top of the trough. Strap the soaked foam into each container, taking the tape right over the trough and foam, with tape ends overlapping. Two straps to each trough will ensure stability.

2 · Divide the lilies, foliage and sweet rocket into two groups. Look to see if the lily stems and rhododendron sprays curve to the right or left and allocate accordingly.

3 · Establish the tallest flower stem on each side, choosing a lily with one or two buds. They should come about to the bar of the cross and no higher. Remember also that you are making a 'mirror-image' group on each side of the arrangement; the buds and flowers on opposite sides should face in opposite directions, either towards each other, or away. This need not be slavishly followed, but if generally applied, the arrangements will look balanced.

4 · Place the longest horizontal line away from the cross on each side with a spray of rhododendron leaves. Use these sprays and the hosta leaves to cover most of the mechanics and mask the rim of the containers with forward-flowing leaves. Remember that you can insert stems into the *sides* of the floral foam as well as into the top of it.

5 · Distribute the remaining lilies through the design, cutting off single open flowers with enough stem to use low down in the arrangement while the buds are used on longer stems. To soften the bold shapes just a little, intersperse a few stems of sweet rocket to break up large dark areas of leaf.

6 · Now walk to the back of the church, turning to look at the arrangement at several places on the way. Judge if the two sides look balanced. Half-close your eyes and the white flowers will show up boldly while the dark greenery will look like areas of black. Are the flowers well distributed? Go back and make any necessary adjustments.

7 · Top up with water but do not overfill or you could mark the altar cloth. Be absolutely meticulous about clearing away bits. Check the floor and straighten cloths before leaving.

Checking the Arrangement

● Arrangers may be required to use the church's own altar vases, often of brass with very narrow necks, but here the arranger has been able to use her own. As this cross is not more than 75 cm (30 in) high, the shallow dishes make it easier to create a low massed arrangement that still leaves the cross as the predomi-nating feature.

● With lilies there is the problem of what to do about the pollen. The orange stain is virtually impossible to remove from pale fabrics and so can mark the altar frontal and cloths (and the whiteness of the flower's own trumpet). Some arrangers cut off the anthers before the pollen ripens and is shed, but this does admittedly destroy much of the beauty of the flower when seen close to. At the altar, however,

where the flowers are seen mainly from a distance, and this factor is therefore unimportant, the solution may be to remove them.
● Now that many altars are being moved away from the reredos and used as a table, with the clergy facing the congregation and

officiating from behind, flowers *on* the altar pose problems. Either they must be kept low or they must be moved away altogether. It is then most usual to have a pedestal arrangement placed nearby. For details of pedestals, see pages 46–7 and 119.

Other Options

Lilies may not always be available or affordable, though in spring the white arum lily (*Zantedeschia aethiopica*) or the yellow (*Z. elliottiana*) are usually easy to obtain. In summer the true

Madonna lily (*Lilium candidum*) may come from a nearby cottage garden or the market. Modern hybrids, in a wide range of colours, most of them bold and very beautiful, are available throughout most of the year.

Although lilies have a special majesty which no other flower can quite match for altar work, large cabbage roses, gerberas, rhododendrons, peonies, daffodils chrysanthemums, dahlias and anthuriums are all distinctive enough in form to be very suitable.

Foliage should not be too small or fussy; even variegated leaves can look confused from the back of the church. It is generally better to use plain green (whether light lime green or dark pine green depends largely on the background) as a foil to the flowers.

CHURCH WINDOWS

Flower decorations on church window sills are often needed for the major festivals of the year and for weddings. The problem of the sloping sill can soon be overcome by having a wedge or small shelf made, to provide a platform for the flower container. Whether the window is of clear or stained glass, the light will be coming from behind the flowers during the day so that the flower arrangement will be silhouetted against it. The choice is between a fairly dense background of leaves or a lacy silhouette to show off the principal flowers.

OVERALL SIZE (W×H)
75 × 90 cm (30 × 36 in)

YOU WILL NEED
Round container or trough about 25 cm (10 in) wide

MECHANICS
Block of soaked floral foam protruding at least 5 cm (2 in) above the rim of the container, secured with sticky tape

PLANT MATERIAL
5–7 sprays of green beech (Fagus sylvestris)

5 stems yellow or variegated leaves

5 sprays berberis or cotoneaster

Ferns (Polystichum setiferum 'Divisilobum') and hart's tongue (Phyllitis scolopendrium)

Hosta leaves

Ivy (Hedera canariensis)

2 white September daisies (Aster ericoides)

5 blue delphiniums

5 yellow lilies

10 red roses ('Baroness' used here)

5–10 red spray carnations

ARRANGER
Jenny Coxhead

This stained glass window has a very steeply sloping sill, but the church handyman had made a platform, which was secured to a ventilation grill below the window. Because the slope is so steep, most of the arrangement will be *below* the window and much of it seen against the stonework rather than the glass.

1 · The first picture shows the platform and the bowl with a large block of soaked foam securely taped in.

2 · An outline of sprays of green beech sets the limits of the arrangement. Avoid covering the stained glass as far as possible. The 'central' stem of beech goes in front of the stone mullion.

3 · Add more foliage, including the hart's tongue ferns, which will give an interesting change of shape from the finer leaves.

4 · A few stems of the dainty white September daisy provide another contrasting shape.

5 · The flower colours have been chosen to echo those in the stained glass. Blue delphiniums should be placed to emphasize the triangular outline made by the first beech leaves.

6 · Choosing the smaller flowers (and longest stems) for the top of the design, put in the five yellow lilies in a broken vertical line through the centre of the arrangement. Have the larger flowers well down on shorter stems.

7 · Add the red roses throughout the design, balancing the colour as well as possible without having them exactly equal on either side. Add a few stems of the red spray carnations if necessary. Top up the container with water. Here it is possible to mist-spray the whole arrangement to help to keep it fresh and moist, without marking the surroundings.

Checking the Arrangement

● Whether to back the flowers with a fairly solid screen of leaves or to settle for a more open outline depends a good deal on what plant material is being used. If colour is important, then a backing is probably needed, but if leaf or flower sprays are attractive in outline and colour is less important, let the decoration be in silhouette.

● Climbing up and down steps (and it should be a step-ladder, not a wobbly chair) to decorate high windows is tiring and increases the risk of accident, so it is often sensible to do most of the arranging on a nearby table. At the start try out the design just once *in situ* to get the height and width right. When the arrangement is nearly done, get someone to help you up with the container

to finish. Make final adjustments because of the altered viewing angle, and top up with water.

Other Options

Because the window sill was so steep here, a central arrangement was the only practical answer. But if a sill is level there is the choice of a central arrangement or one at each side, or a border of flowers

and foliage arranged as a frieze along the whole length, possibly with downward trailing sprays and flowers (as for the font on page 113) or as a grouping of parallels in the European manner (see page 23). If flowers are to be placed at each end of the window embrasure, it usually means that they are backed by the side walls of the alcove and will not obscure too much of the glass and light.

THE FONT

The circular top of the font is usually decorated only for a christening or a special church festival. For either occasion the font's very purpose suggests that the flower decoration should be simple and unsophisticated, using small flowers in mainly pastel colours and white. The mechanics for a garland can be purchased ready-made or can be home-made. Some churches have special trough containers made to fit the font, but these are often too deep and are difficult to arrange well.

OVERALL SIZE
Circular, inner diameter about 50 cm (20 in)

YOU WILL NEED
Thick polythene sheeting to protect the surface, with 10 cm- (4 in-) wide sections cut to make a 50 cm (20 in) circle

3 shallow troughs or trays if flowers are to be put at base

MECHANICS
10–12 sections commercial garland-maker filled with soaked floral foam – or 2 large blocks of soaked floral foam

Cling film

2 cm (¾ in) wire mesh

Block of soaked floral foam if flowers to be put at base

Green sticky tape

PLANT MATERIAL
Short stems and sprays of a dainty foliage such as cupressus, box, hellebore, small hostas, peony, Acer platanoides 'Drummondii', ivies

Longer trails of variegated ivy

Variety of pastel-coloured flowers such as delphinium, hellebores, freesias, spray carnations and chrysanthemums, roses, sprays of spiraea, gypsophila, penstemons

ARRANGER
Beryl Rose

1 · If the decoration is for an actual christening, a good space must be left at the back for the vicar/priest and the baby. For a flower festival it is usual to complete the circular decoration, but it is sensible to make a removable section in case it is needed.

2 · To make your own version of the hook-together cages of commercial garland-maker, cut the two large blocks of floral foam into 16 pieces, each 10 × 5 × 4 cm (4 × 2 × 1½ in). Wrap these pieces of floral foam in cling film like a string of sausages, and encase them in 2 cm (¾ in) wire mesh.

3 · Lay the sections of thick polythene on the top of the font, overlapping them to make sure it is well protected. Place the garland of floral foam 'sausages' on top of this. It should have been soaked beforehand and allowed to drain well so that it does not drip.

4 · Begin by covering as much of the foam as possible with single leaves and short sprigs of foliage, using longer sprays of ivy and spiraea at intervals to trail down gracefully from the top. Don't overdo the trailing pieces or the decoration will soon begin to look top-heavy.

5 · Now intersperse the flowers, mixing the colours casually. Aim for a balanced but not rigidly symmetrical look.

6 · As more water cannot be added to the foam, mist-spray the garland to reduce water loss. Be sure to clear all the bits out of the font basin.

7 · The decoration here has been finished with a crescent of flowers and foliage repeated at the base of the font. This is entirely optional and may depend on whether the font is on a raised platform. The crescent is arranged in three small shallow troughs filled with soaked foam, taped in securely. Make quite sure that the base arrangements will not get in the way of people's feet.

Checking the Arrangement

● Although a good effect can be achieved with far fewer flowers than have been used here, you need enough to avoid a spotty, or too equally spaced, look.
● Foliage with white, cream or yellow variegation can help to make the flowers go further.
● Because so many short-stemmed flowers and leaves are used, garlanding a font can be very time-consuming so, if possible, have a helper with you, even if it is only to sort out the flowers and foliage and prepare short pieces.

Other Options

In early spring a charming decoration can be made with small clumps of primroses, violets, polyanthus, crocus, forsythia, small daffodils and grape hyacinths arranged in damp sphagnum moss, or in little pots hidden in the moss.

In autumn small pom-pom dahlias and spray chrysanthemums with michaelmas daisies are just as effective.

The creams and browns of dried and preserved leaves and flowers, however, never look right for a christening, though for a flower festival they can sometimes be linked with a carved wooden font cover.

POT-ET-FLEUR

The term 'pot-et-fleur' (literally 'pot and flower') was coined in 1960 to describe an arrangement of growing rooted plants with some cut flowers added to give additional colour and interest. The plants can remain in their pots or be planted out in a container of good potting compost, with gravel or broken crocks at the bottom to provide drainage. The plants alone should provide a pleasing group, even without the cut flowers, so the decoration is long-lasting and with care can last for several years. Flowers can be added or replaced as needed.

OVERALL SIZE (W × H)

75 cm × 2 m (30 × 80 in) including plinth

YOU WILL NEED

Large deep plastic urn/bowl painted to look like stone, raised on a plinth

MECHANICS

3 florist's plastic cones and pieces of soaked floral foam to fit them

PLANT MATERIAL

Howeia fosteriana *(Kentia palm) for height*

Rhoicissus rhombifolia *(trailing left)*

Calathea picturata *'Vandenheckie' (variegated leaves on right)*

Begonia elatior *'Aphrodite' (at back left, in flower)*

Begonia rex *(grey/pink leaves centre front)*

Hedera *– any variety (back left)*

Moss to fill in gaps

Flowers: 3 pink lilies, 5 alstroemeria, 10 carnations

ARRANGER

Barbara Weight

1 · Choose a container deep enough and large enough to take the plant pots and leave space for plastic cones or small containers

for the cut flowers. To save space, one or two of the smaller plants can be de-potted into a plastic bag with a few holes cut for drainage. (This was done here for the ivy and begonia.)

2 · Position the tallest plant (Kentia palm) towards the back, raising it on an upturned flower pot if more height is needed. Try to have the tallest stem at least twice the height of the container.

3 · Place the trailing plant (*Rhoicissus rhombifolia*) to the left towards the front and the variegated leaf plant (*Calathea picturata*) to the right.

4 · Add the flowering plant (*Begonia elatior*) towards the back left to give depth to the arrangement, the ivy (hedera) to the back right and the colourful *Begonia rex* a little off-centre at the front.

5 · 'Plant' one plastic-cone flower holder filled with soaked floral foam in front of and to the left of the tallest plant, one to the right behind the calathea and one low down in the front left of the *Begonia rex*. Ensure that they are mostly hidden by foliage, and that they are topped up with water before starting to arrange, as cones are so easily forgotten when watering afterwards.

6 · Arrange the tallest lily with its bud just above the palm and the others on graduated shorter stems filling the space on the left. Add alstroemeria if needed to fill gaps.

7 · Use the carnations in a tight group on the right and five at the front coming forward over the rhoicissus.

8 · Tuck in moss to hide any pots or flower holders, and be sure that every pot has adequate water. A misting spray of water helps to reduce evaporation.

Checking the Arrangement

● The growing plants are the mainstay of a pot-et-fleur and their grouping should be sufficiently pleasing that they could remain without flowers.

● As the container is inevitably large and deep, it is important to achieve enough height with the tallest plant. A dumpy pot-et-fleur lacks elegance and good proportions.

● For a church decoration, where possibly a number of different people will be watering and attending to the pot-et-fleur, it is better to leave the plants in their pots. If one plant dies, it is then a simple job to replace it.

● To help those who will top up later, include an inconspicuous label saying how many flower cones there are.

Other Options

With the large range of foliage and flowering house-plants available today, there are many alternatives to the plants used here. Look at those sold by local garden centres, supermarkets or florists.

You will need one or two plants from each of the following categories in order to give variety and interest:

Tall: Ivy (hedera) trained up a mossy pole, mother-in-law's tongue (*Sansevieria trifasciata*), dracaena, schefflera.

Bushy: Ferns including maidenhair (adiantum) and davallia, umbrella grass (cyperus), silk oak (*Grevillea robusta*), croton (*Codiaeum variegatum*), ctenanthe, euonymus, fittonia, maranta, selaginella.

Flowering: Azalea, begonia, chrysanthemum, cyclamen, hydrangea, kalanchoë, pelargonium, poinsettia (*Euphorbia pulcherrima*) or primula.

Trailing: *Asparagus plumosus*, spider plant (chlorophytum), columnea, nephrolepsis, pilea, trandescantia.

PEW ENDS

For flower festivals, weddings and special occasions, pew-end decorations are inexpensive and yet do more than any other arrangements to give the effect of a church filled with flowers, because they are right among the congregation. The shape of the top of the pew will dictate what mechanics should be used, but the handled plastic tray of foam can be adapted to suit most shapes. It is seldom necessary to put decorations on every pew down the central aisle; flowers on alternate ones are effective. If the aisle is narrow, keep them quite small or the choir will crush the flowers with their robes!

OVERALL SIZE (W × H)
23 × 60 cm (9 × 24 in)

YOU WILL NEED
Wreath tray with handle

MECHANICS
Block of soaked floral foam
Green sticky tape (unless foam is already 'caged')
Silver reel wire

PLANT MATERIAL
4–5 sprays yew
5 leaves tansy (Tanacetum vulgare)
3 variegated hosta leaves
5 white dendrobium orchids
Small white flowers such as gypsophila, September flower (Aster ericoides) or bouvardia
Bunch of lily-of-the-valley (Convallaria)
2 sprays single white chrysanthemums
2 stems yellow lilies

ACCESSORIES
Pale yellow or cream waterproof 'tearable' ribbon 5 cm (2 in) wide

ARRANGER
Jenny Coxhead

1 · Strap the soaked [...] tray firmly if there is [...] cage around it. Up-en[...] and allow it to drain [...] excess water, or it can [...] the arrangement is in [...] some newspaper is pla[...] the tray.

2 · Lay the tray flat on [...] surface and arrange the [...] sprays of yew. (It is sho[...] position on the pew for [...] tive purposes.)

3 · Continue covering the foam with tansy and hosta leaves. Remember that when in place, the sides and top end of the tray will be visible and foliage should therefore cover them.

scarce or expensive, use more variegated foliage.

5 · Use the lilies for central interest in a gentle line running down from top to bottom.

6 · For weddings and festivals, ribbon trails look pretty. These are made by tearing lengths of ribbon into 1 cm- (½ in-) wide strips and pulling them sharply over the back of a knife to make them curl. (The firmer the pull the tighter the curl. Repeat the process on the reverse of the ribbon to straighten it out and loosen the curl.) Twist a stub wire around several ribbons at one end to make a long 'stem' to insert into the foam.

Other Options

There are a number of alternative fixings for pew ends. One of the most popular is the commercial half round of foam in a plastic cage on a large clip to go over the top of the pew. (This was not suitable for the pews pictured here.) The size of the foam – 8 cm (3 in) in diameter – only allows for a smaller decoration.

If the pew end has a level top, a container can be made from a sardine tin glued to a narrow strip of wood that has two 'terry' clips nailed underneath to clip over the pew upright. Alternatively, cut polystyrene food trays to size and attach long hooks made from tape-covered stub wires to hook over the pew ends. The polystyrene backing protects the woodwork and provides a base on which to tape a piece of soaked foam wrapped in cling film.

With a straight-topped pew end the shape of the arrangement can vary. It looks good if the widest part is at the top, tapering to a point.

Plant materials can obviously change with the seasons. The size of the decoration may need to be reduced because flowers are less plentiful. At Christmas a red, white and green colour scheme can easily be built up with evergreens and florists' flowers, such as red spray chrysanthemums. Avoid using prickly holly, as people will brush close to the flowers. Rosemary, box and plainer green leaves of skimmia or choisya make a good combination of foliage. Not all churches like ribbons, except for weddings, so check what is acceptable. While it is never possible, and certainly not desirable, to have every pew end exactly matching, as though turned out on a conveyer belt, it is sensible for an overall harmonious look to have much the same flowers and foliage in each decoration.

7 · Split a length of ribbon in two and tie it to the handle of the tray then tie this to the pew end. Finish it off on the pew side with a ribbon bow held in place with silver wire.

Checking the Arrangement

Take care that the arrangement does not protrude too far into a narrow aisle and that any ribbons clear the floor and people's feet.

CHAPTER SEVEN · REVIEW

*C*hurch flower arrangements must be bold enough to be seen from a distance, and should incorporate advancing or pale colours to show up well in dim light. They also need to be carefully positioned so that they do not interfere with church services. In order to last through the whole week, the flowers must be very well chosen and conditioned.

What You'll Need

The opening to the chapter suggested what a new church flower arranger should know before starting out. Here is a checklist of what to take:

TOOLS AND EQUIPMENT

Flower cutters and/or secateurs
Cloth for spills and duster
Misting spray and long-spouted watering can
Drop sheet for rubbish and to protect the floor (you can also carry foliage in this)
Plastic rubbish bag
Brush and dustpan (unless you are certain they are in the church)

MECHANICS

Block(s) and/or rounds of floral foam
Tape to secure foam in container (or crumpled wire mesh and reel wire to tie it in)
Plastic cones and garden canes if needed for a very tall arrangement
Container(s) if church ones not being used

PLANT MATERIALS

Well-conditioned foliage
Long-lasting flowers, also well conditioned

TRANSPORT

Take long-stemmed flowers and foliage in a flower box lined with thin polythene or standing in a bucket part-filled with water.

Single leaves travel well in a polythene bag closed with a wire twist.
If you are walking to the church, it is better to take flowers and foliage in a handled bucket with a little water, than in a basket or a trug.

Conditioning of Plant Material

As church arrangements are often expected to last through a whole week (decorators tend to re-do the flowers on the day before the Sabbath), the choice and conditioning of flowers and leaves is extremely important. Flowers should be picked or bought the day before they are needed and left in deep water in buckets in a cool place for 24 hours. Young spring foliage needs the boiling-water treatment as well (see page 14) and most woody stemmed material (flowers, foliage and berries) will also benefit from it.

Containers

Church flower containers are often very unsuitable for present-day arrangements, and narrow-necked brass altar vases are perhaps the most difficult. However, it is usually possible (and allowed) to fix a candlecup into them, and with floral foam (now the usual mechanics) a sizeable arrangement can be created.

For larger containers, there is a wide range of plastic urns, boxes, bowls and troughs sold by garden centres for patio use. These can easily be adapted by painting or spraying them to look like stone (see page 115) or like marble or brass so that they fit into their surroundings. It is important that containers look good, not trashy, so painting and adapting must be done well.

Styles of Arrangement

Because many church buildings are old and traditional with a good deal of space and height, arrangements tend to be massed with fairly solid groups of flowers and leaves so that they show up well.

The tall pedestal arrangement has always been popular because it is raised up some 90 to 120 cm (36 to 48 in) on a column, plinth or wrought-iron stand and can be seen at a distance. (See the pedestal arrangement on page 47.) There is also the advantage that the stand can be moved from one part of the building to another as occasion demands and so is particularly versatile.

On the other hand, in recent years there has been a good deal of interest in arrangements on the floor! The parallel verticals of flowers and foliage grouped together in blocks of one type and one colour in the European style have made a great impact in many church festivals. There is an excellent example on page 153. The same rules about size and boldness still apply, but because the plant materials are already in blocks of one colour, the *effect* of larger blooms and leaves is already achieved.

Using Dried and Preserved Materials

More thought could be given to using dried and gly-cerined material in church arrangements. During the winter months they can provide a long-lasting frame-work, to which a few bold fresh flowers, such as chrysanthemums, lilies or gerberas can be added.

Chapter Eight

COMPETITIVE SHOWS

People are often surprised that flower arrangement shows (in Western countries at least) are usually competitive. This is a natural development from their origins in the classes for 'flowers arranged for effect' at horticultural shows, which have always had a strong competitive element. While competition may seem strange for a hobby accepted as a minor art form, the seeking of prizes and trophies and, more importantly, the acclaim and prestige that go with them, is still practised in music, literature and art.

or flower arrangers competitive work is an opportunity to show off in public what is usually practised at home, and a chance to measure their ability and artistry against those of others. Because extra effort and a good deal of thought go into a show exhibit, the experience is a valuable one. Even without a prize or commendation there is the card with the judge's comments as guidance for future exhibits.

Schedules

At first, show schedules would simply ask for a bowl or vase of flowers arranged for effect and the emphasis was on artistry rather than horticultural perfection.

Then some setting began to be referred to: 'an arrangement for the hall', 'for a dark corner' or 'for a guest's bedside table'. An additional element had crept in, for not only were the flowers to be decorative but they had to be suitable for a particular place and purpose. If the 'dark corner' was the class in question, it was no good thinking in terms of blues and purples!

This led, gradually, to more and more *interpretation* being called for in flower arrangement classes, with titles such as 'Spring Beauty' or 'Autumn Glory'. These were not too difficult, but 'Spring Fever' called for more thought and 'Spring Cleaning' for some accessories, perhaps.

Today, world-wide, most flower arrangement shows have a title for each class. Many are elaborate and challenging, such as: 'Quintessence', 'Man of Action', 'Make Believe', 'Art Trouvé'.

Or the arrangements might have to interpret a quotation, such as 'If there were dreams to sell, what would you buy?'

Entering your First Show

● Read the schedule carefully. If special rules or definitions are referred to, be sure to get a copy of those as well. Most shows in Britain are judged by the *NAFAS Handbook of Schedule Definitions*. (The latest issue, at the time of going to press, is the 8th, which came into force in 1988.) Other organizations (such as the Royal Horticultural Society, The World Association of Flower Arrangers, the Women's Institutes, the Society of Floristry) and most other countries have their own rules. If there is anything you do not understand, ask the Show Secretary.
● Do any necessary homework. Look up class title words in a dictionary or thesaurus. Consult a book of quotations if necessary. These may give you ideas or alternative meanings to consider.
● Think what plant materials may be available to you at the time of the show, in your own or friends' gardens, at the florist's, garden centre or nursery. Can any of the flowers, leaves or fruits help your interpretation with their colour, shape, line or texture? For example, vines and fruit will suggest harvest, plenty, autumn, the good life; thorns, spear-shaped leaves, and rough textures will suggest war, poverty, famine; yellow and green are the colours of spring, youth, sunshine, Easter.
● Consider a possible container, base, background or accessory. How can each of these be made to play a useful part?
● Have one or two try-outs and mock-ups *within the space allowed*. Make good use of the space, but don't over-fill it and don't exceed it. Select what is best and firmly reject the rest. You can never use all the ideas that you have thought of, so the important word is '*select*'.
● There is no right or wrong way to interpret any class title. A dozen exhibitors may all see it quite differently. That's what makes shows so interesting. What matters is that the message is clear to the judge and to the visitors and that the exhibit is well designed and immaculately presented, with the emphasis on the plant material telling the story.

Accessories

Accessories used in flower arrangement exhibits are those items that are not natural plant material, such as stones, shells, feathers, candles, figurines, books, fabric.

Unless a particular show schedule says otherwise, containers holding plant material, mechanics, bases, backgrounds and exhibit titles are not considered accessories and may be used at any time.

In competitive work accessories should never dominate the plant material. Be very selective about them and try to incorporate them with the plant materials rather than dotting them around.

Many overseas arrangers think that the British rely far too much on accessories to bolster up interpretative exhibits at shows and festivals. Most judges would agree that it is indeed a tendency that needs watching. The arranger's medium is plant material, and one who really learns and understands what is available at any time of year need never rely on gimmicky accessories.

A First Show Entry

It is sensible to enter a novice or beginners' class at your first show. The class title is not likely to be too complicated, the space allowed is generally not daunting and your fellow competitors will have only limited experience in competitive work. Concentrate on a style of arrangement you feel at home with. Make sure you will be able to get from your own or friends' gardens and the florist the sort of flowers and leaves that will be suitable to interpret the class title. Here it is 'Summer Opulence'.

OVERALL SIZE (W × D × H)
75 × 55 × 90 cm (30 × 21 × 36 in)

YOU WILL NEED
Low-stemmed bowl

MECHANICS
Block of soaked floral foam to fit bowl
'Frog' and putty-type adhesive, or sticky tape

PLANT MATERIAL
2 tall iris leaves
10–12 hosta leaves
7 stems blue delphiniums
About 15 open roses – included here are Rosa mundi *(striped),* 'Constance Spry', 'Iceberg' *and others*
8 stems alchemilla
Several stems honeysuckle

ARRANGER
Judy Routledge

1 · Look up 'opulence' in the dictionary and discover that it means 'abundance, riches, wealth, luxury, even ostentation'. Add to that the word 'summer' and the title suggests all the richness and abundance of high summer in the garden. The rose perhaps typifies this more than any other flower.

2 · Having decided that the rose is to be the main flower, the arranger's next step is to determine the style of the arrangement. Sensibly, she chose to do a symmetrical triangle, which she felt happy with and which would look massed and abundant.

3 · As roses were unlikely to provide the full height needed, either foliage or other flowers had to be chosen. A show exhibit should make full use of the height allocated, so that in a space 90 cm (36 in) high the longest stem needs to be 85 cm (33–34 in) tall. A slightly raised container will help with this. Iris leaves and delphiniums have been selected here for that reason.

4 · Hosta leaves will help establish the width. Again the whole width should be used, but comfortably, with a margin of space which acts like a frame around the arrangement.

5 · Once the soaked floral foam is taped into the container, height is established with the two iris leaves at the centre back, one a little shorter than the other. The curving tips give a gentle off-centre variation to the ramrod-straight 'backbone' more usually associated with the iris.

6 · Delphinium flowers strengthen this central spine and are taken down to the left hand side. Hosta leaves mark the width and some with longer stems set an outline from top to side placements.

7 · Roses are put in next, with the paler colours ranging down the left, helping to balance the leaf-tips curving right. The slightly darker *Rosa mundi* is grouped on the right. The largest blooms are used centrally. Gaps are filled with heads of alchemilla and a few trails of honeysuckle.

8 · Wisely the arranger has omitted any accessories. Nothing further was needed to help the interpretation and nothing extra was needed for balance. Even the small base that was tried and then removed was not needed with an arrangement that sat comfortably in its alloted space.

Checking the Arrangement

● It is always important to make sure that the back of the arrangement is well finished and not looking stalky and flat. There should be almost as much depth from the tallest stem backwards as there is towards the front. This is especially important where an exhibit, like this one, is at the end of a class and can easily be seen from one side by the judge and the public. This is just the luck of the draw, but it should not be overlooked.
● It is to be hoped that the container was well filled before the exhibit was left for judging and that all bits were flicked or blown away from the base.

Other Options

The arranger could have decided to go for a wide range of summer flowers of all colours, shapes and sizes to suggest the 'wealth' required. There is always more

than one way of interpreting a title, but the important thing is that it can be understood by the judge and the visitors.

To fit in with the title 'Opulence' various containers could be chosen, such as a gilded urn or a figurine supporting a bowl or an ornately decorated box.

These could have been staged on some rich fabric (velvet, satin, brocade) with perhaps golden tassels and cord at the foot of the container. Lilies and carnations might have been included as well as a separate dish of summer fruits including peaches, apricots and strawberries.

A landscape design is possible, suggesting a garden with mixed and massed summer flowers, paving stones or an archway of flowers. But for one's first show exhibit it is sensible to play safe and concentrate on having well-conditioned plant material and everything immaculately staged.

AN INTERMEDIATE EXHIBIT

Though not all shows have them, intermediate classes do provide a chance for the exhibitor who has won prizes as a novice to attempt something a little more challenging. Here the exhibitor has used a painted background and base, two separate placements of plant material and one or two accessories. For a class called 'Far-away Places' she chose to interpret 'On the Edge of Paradise' and concentrated on creating the feel of tropical warmth and plentiful vegetation.

OVERALL SIZE (W ×D ×H)
75 × 70 × 90 cm (30 × 27 × 36 in)

YOU WILL NEED
Plywood or equivalent for background and bases
Piece of stripped ivy screwed to a second, thinner base
Emulsion and acrylic paint
2 small dishes

MECHANICS
2 Lok-joint fittings, screwdriver
Screw-in candlecup
1 round and 2 small pieces of soaked floral foam
Cocktail sticks/toothpicks

PLANT MATERIAL
Fruit: plums, apples, kiwi fruit, peaches, small pineapple, plums
6 cerise dendrobium orchid sprays
6 pink gerberas
2 lilies ('Red Knight' used here)
4 pink anthuriums
Large seedheads, purple leaves of hebe and heuchera, purple statice flowers
Glycerined eucalyptus leaves
4 echeveria rosettes

ACCESSORIES
Vine pot, 2 shells

ARRANGER
Germaine Smith

1 · Arrangers find a background and base very useful for show work. This 'tombstone' shape, as it is often called, is cut from plywood and is just under 90 cm (36 in) high by 75 cm (30 in) wide, in order to fit within the show space dimensions that are generally popular. The base board is also curved at the front and is about 60 cm (24 in) from back to front. The two boards can be carried flat and joined together at the show bench with two screw-down fittings which join the boards at right angles. These are called 'Lok-joints' and are obtainable at do-it-yourself shops and hardware stores. Once the boards have been made they can be painted, sprayed or covered with fabric, to suit the demands of any class.

2 · Here the boards have been painted to suggest sea and sky with a distant horizon, so that the whole exhibit looks like an island. It is very important to avoid too much detail in the background. It should not attract attention, but remain what it is, a background to enhance the plant material.

3 · The piece of stripped ivy that supports the top arrangement is screwed into a secondary base, and the weight of the flowers, fruit and accessories makes it quite stable. A screw-in candle-cup is fitted to the top of the ivy branch. Tape a round of soaked foam into the candlecup and the pieces of foam into the two small dishes. These are then placed on the base on either side of the ivy branch, towards the back.

4 · The vine-bound pot and two shells are grouped to the left of the stripped ivy. The fruit is now put into position, and anchored where necessary with cocktail sticks/toothpicks. The kiwi fruits are cut open to display their colour and pattern.

5 · Put in the orchids next – their graceful sprays are a very necessary contrast to the generally round shapes of fruit and flowers. On the left at the top and on the right at the bottom, they lead the eye downwards in a gentle curve. Include the eucalyptus leaves with them.

6 · Three pink gerberas in the top arrangement and at the bottom act as a focal point for each group. Back them up with the orange lilies and the pink anthuriums. Put in the large seedheads, purple hebe and heuchera leaves and dark purple statice to add depth to the whole design.

7 · Finally, the group of echeveria in the front (which do not, even under competition rules, need to be in water) gives a different shape and a soft colour link between the base and shells.

Checking the Arrangement

The good points in this exhibit include:
● the use of 'hot' colours, without green foliage to cool them down, to give a tropical feel
● the attractive asymmetrical balance
● the well painted, only-just-suggested seascape background

● the inclusion of fruits suggesting abundance

● the use of accessories within, and as part of, the arrangement.

Other Options

Bearing in mind that this exhibit was in a class entitled 'Far-away Places', the possibilities are endless (which indicates that it was a good class title). Exhibitors could interpret the frozen north, the orient, desert oases, rain forests, Shangri-la, the golden road to Samarkand, and so on.

The important factor would be to find plant material that interpreted the chosen place. This might be done with plants that actually grow there or with similar forms or colour. Accessories can certainly help but they should always be in a supporting role to the plant material. They should never be allowed to dominate the arrangement at all.

AN ISLAND SITE

Island sites are appearing more and more at shows and give the arranger additional problems because the exhibit is seen (and usually judged) from all around. There must therefore be interest and balance from all viewpoints. Platforms are usually 90, 122 or 152 cm (36, 48 or 60 in) in diameter, or square, and raised about 30 cm (12 in) from the floor. The height of the exhibit is often 'unlimited', and it is staging a good height in proportion to the space allowed that most frequently causes difficulty.

OVERALL SIZE (W×H)
110×230 cm (42×90 in)

THE ARRANGER USED
Very large piece of driftwood or smaller pieces screwed together
Lead dish 60 cm (24 in) across
1–2 large pieces of rough stone

MECHANICS
4 plastic dishes, plastic tray
5 small blocks of soaked floral foam, green sticky tape, putty-type adhesive

ACCESSORY
Carved stone head

PLANT MATERIAL
Hosta leaves (including some variegated)
Sprays of Cornus alba *and Solomon's seal*
Ivy trails, honeysuckle, moss
Striped grass
10 pink lilies
15 'Champagne' roses
15 'Bridal Pink' roses
Alstroemeria
10 spray carnations
Astrantia
4 stems spray chrysanthemums
Stocks, 10 larkspur

ARRANGER
Christine Churchward

This and the following exhibit both use wood to gain height, and they both interpret 'Rendezvous' but in very different ways.

1 · As 'Rendezvous' means either 'an appointed meeting place' or 'a meeting by appointment', the arranger here imagined a lovers' tryst by a pool; the adoring lover lies at his lady's feet.

2 · Constructing and setting up the driftwood is the first and hardest task. This large piece is screwed to a lump of bog oak for weight and stability and has an extra leg screwed on at the left to provide balance. Another piece stretches across the lead dish, with a stone prop underneath. The dish is easily home-made from a piece of sheet lead bought at a builders' merchant. Cut to a roughly rounded shape with tin snips, the sides – about 4 cm (1½ in) high – are hammered up against a wood block.

3 · Three dishes holding soaked foam are secured with tape and putty-type adhesive to the main driftwood: one at the top, one halfway up on the left and one behind, lower down. A fourth dish of foam is to the right on the stone, and a fifth foam block is held on a 'frog' to the left of the lead dish.

4 · Prop the stone head in the dish so that the features can be seen, and begin to arrange hosta leaves in the dishes and foam as in the first picture.

5 · Make the apparently continuous curve of flowers and foliage with long sprays of *Cornus alba* and Solomon's seal coming down from the top dish, up and down from the middle one and up from the back. Follow the line of the curve with pink lilies.

6· Continue the line with well-spaced flowers: roses, alstroemeria, spray carnations, astrantia, chrysanthemums (the darker pinkish-red), stocks and larkspur.

7· Fill in with ivy, honeysuckle and moss. Complete the little group in the pool with grasses and a few flowers but with little colour, letting the sweep of colour run down to the right-hand side.

Checking the Arrangement

It is difficult with an island site to be sure that plant material (especially from a high placement) does not extend beyond the base, so it is quite common to have schedule wording which states: 'to be staged on a four foot diameter base and within a five foot square'. This allows some latitude and helps to avoid disqualification from having 'exceeded the space allowed' with, say, a trail of ivy. It also allows the exhibit to look better than if it is rigidly confined within the base platform.

Other Options

The theme 'Rendezvous' could be interpreted in the same way at almost any time of the year, as no specific plant material is called for, except perhaps a few waterside plants for the pool.

The driftwood arrangement can suggest a beautiful lady in any range of pretty flowers and soft colours, which can be based on yellow, white or blue as well as pink, or a mixture of pastels.

The next page shows another interpretation of the same title in a bolder style, but the possibilities of other rendezvous are infinite – for example, the breakthrough in the Channel Tunnel, Stanley and Livingstone meeting in Africa, or the great gathering of pilgrims at Canterbury.

ANOTHER RENDEZVOUS

Whereas the interpretation on pages 126–7 relied on a 'story' to tell, this exhibit is all about design and colour and two delightful accessories meeting centre-stage, but not dominating the two groups of plant material. The mirror-image arrangements in similar pots make their own rendezvous of patterns, and their colouring makes the link with the fabric. Each type of plant material is grouped together in European continental style, perhaps suggesting another meeting-place for Britain with Europe.

OVERALL SIZE (W×H)
120 × 210 cm (48 × 84 in)

YOU WILL NEED
Circular chipboard base 105cm (42 in) in diameter, painted blue-grey
Sturdy branches of stripped ivy cut to make a stand about 120 cm (48 in) high, screwed to a small base and a circular top, all painted blue-grey
Wire basket with handles
3 m (3¼ yd) fabric in abstract design of navy, red and orange
2 large glazed blue pots, one rounder than the other

MECHANICS
Block of soaked floral foam taped in the top of both pots

PLANT MATERIAL
15 large dried poppy seedheads
10 fatsia leaves
4 stems blue cedar
5 orange lilies
7 blue and 2 mauve delphiniums
6 dried stems (from the poppies)
12 orange carnations

ACCESSORIES
2 carved wooden swans

ARRANGER
Bett Wareing

1 · Position the stand centrally on the base and hook the basket handle over the stand. Taking hold of one corner and taping it to the flat top, drape the fabric from the top of the stand over the ivy, into and out of the basket, down to the base, where it is bunched and finishes in a swirl on the floor. (This would cause disqualification if the show schedule did not allow a space greater than the diameter of the base.)

2 · Place the tallest pot on top and the rounder one on the base to the right.

3 · Put the two birds in place so that the balance of shape and colour can be judged. Accessories should always be placed *in situ* early on. They may need to be removed for convenience later on in the arranging, but they should be brought back frequently to ensure that they are really part of the design, not an afterthought.

4 · Half of the poppy seedheads establish the central height in both jars. Add the lilies in a central line coming down to the rim of the containers. The lower pot arrangement is always a slightly smaller, and reversed, version of the top one.

5 · Fatsia leaves are used in a circular sweep from high on the left at the top, and from the right in the bottom container.

6 · Two stems of blue cedar establish diagonals to the left at the top and to the right below. This diagonal line is now exaggerated by blue delphiniums and straight dried stems on the right (top) and left (bottom). Seven stems of orange carnations extend to the left at the top, and five stems to the right at the bottom, continuing the strong diagonal line.

7 · Three short-stemmed poppy heads are grouped between the lilies and carnations in each jar. The poppy heads and the stalks make an important contribution to the design, providing a pale beige link with the two birds.

Checking the Arrangement

● Both this and the 'Rendezvous' exhibit on pages 126–7 use wood to obtain the height needed for good proportions. It is a popular choice as it is natural plant material (even though painted) and so there is no danger that it over-accessorizes the exhibit. But both exhibits do need accessories to some extent. It is not easy to suggest a meeting or meeting-place without some accessories to help the interpretation. The secret is not to overdo them and to choose only those that do the job effectively. It is not necessary to have shells, sand, towel, suntan oil, sun spectacles, bucket and spade to suggest a day at the seaside; the sand and shells would suffice.
● In neither exhibit is colour a powerful factor in the interpretation in the way that yellow and orange flowers and leaves would be for an exhibit entitled 'Golden October'. However, the pink flowers for a

lady in the previous exhibit do echo the well-known 'blue for a boy, pink for a girl' convention. In the exhibit pictured here, colour is a *design* feature: a scheme inspired by the fabric and the crafted birds and carried through in the painted ivy, bases, pots, basket and plant materials.

Other Options

If a different fabric and different accessories were used the design would change and the colours too. Choose a piece of fabric of your own and plan what you would do with it. Or think of another rendezvous to interpret. You should be able to follow your own ideas by now.

Chapter eight · Review

A competitor at any show will be hoping to win a prize or at least a commendation from the judge. That is the purpose of competition. The monetary rewards in flower arrangement shows are seldom considerable, but winning a First Prize ribbon, rosette or spoon, or better still a trophy (for a year), is an achievement to boost one's pride and ego.

What the Judge Looks For

It is sensible to know what the judge is looking for and to keep this firmly in mind when planning and setting up an exhibit.

CONFORMING TO THE SCHEDULE

Competitions have to have some rules, competitors have to abide by them and judges have to judge by them. The *NAFAS Handbook of Schedule Definitions* sets out the simple rules which govern all shows judged in accordance with them. Contravening any of the following points is cause for *disqualification* under the NAFAS system. (Many other countries have rules which call for down-pointing instead.)

(a) Failure to comply with any specific requirements for a class as stated in the show schedule, ie the measurements or the components.

(b) Inclusion of any fresh plant material that does not have its roots or cut ends of its stems in water or water-retaining material. Air plants, cacti, fruits, grass turf, lichen, moss, succulents and vegetables need not conform to this ruling.

(c) Inclusion of artificial plant material (unless specifically allowed by a show schedule).

A judge's first task, therefore, is to check these points, or be assured by the show stewards that a check has been made.

INTERPRETATION OF THE CLASS TITLE

If the class has a title, and most do, then the judge will hope that the interpretation comes over mainly in the plant materials by imaginative use of colours, shapes and textures, or by well-known associations – for example, poppies for World War I, roses or oaks for England, tulips for Holland, ivy for constancy. Accessories should play only a supporting role.

GOOD DESIGN

The exhibit should be well balanced, with items in scale, rhythm running through the composition, enough contrast to make it interesting and above all a harmony of style in the choice of container, accessories, base, etc, as well as in plant materials.

PRESENTATION

The actual staging of the exhibit will be important. The space allowed should be well used, but not crowded; the layout, especially on a large site, should be artistically organized; the finish of the bases, backgrounds, etc, should be immaculate and the whole presentation should be well-groomed. In addition, the judge will be looking for a touch of originality and distinction. Most important of all, the plant material must predominate.

On Show Day

Make up your mind that you are going to *enjoy* entering. Allow plenty of time to get to the show and arrive in good time. Check with the show secretary and find your allocated space. Don't be discouraged if you find yourself working next to someone you know to be infinitely more experienced. Stick to what you have planned.

Remember to keep within your own space; you will not be popular if you lay flowers in your neighbour's niche or take up too much room spreading out buckets and boxes.

Walk away quite frequently from what you have done. Faults in balance or colour grouping show up far more clearly from the other side of the hall/tent.

When nearly finished take a coffee-break and go right away. When you come back, view the exhibit as dispassionately as possible. Finish off, pack up, check water levels, mist-spray if you can and *leave well alone*. Everyone is tempted to fiddle too much.

A Learning Session

Use the show as a valuable classroom. Both during staging (if you can do so without getting in the way of other exhibitors) and afterwards, look at other exhibits and learn from them. It is always easier to find faults in someone else's work than it is to see them in your own, but you will learn to assess good and bad points more easily the more practice you get.

When judging is done and you are allowed back in the hall, the judge may still be writing comment cards on exhibits. Most judges are happy to come and talk about your exhibit if there is time, but even if you have no prize, there will usually be a comment card from the judge. Consider the remarks in relation to your exhibit before it is taken down, and learn from them. Read as many other comments as you can, and you will learn much from them as well.

Not everyone likes to be competitive, but there is something about a show that gets the adrenalin flowing and you can learn more there than in several months at home. The camaraderie between competitors is one of the most unexpected but really great pleasures of flower arranging.

Chapter Nine

LOOKING BACK AT HISTORY

*Period-style flower arrangements are quite often required today.
With the present interest in conservation and the preservation of our heritage,
they can play an important part in historical displays, festivals in historic
houses and stately homes or day-to-day decoration in museums
and art galleries. In seeking to make them as authentic as possible, flower
arrangers learn much about the gardens, plants, colours and
general lifestyle of past ages.*

Evidence of the interest in the past in flowers and leaves for decoration can be seen in contemporary paintings and prints; architecture and plaster work; tomb paintings; furniture inlays and carvings; china, glass and metalwork; fabrics, furnishings and embroidery; tapestries; herbals, essays, diaries, poetry; household accounts; and, from the 19th century on, novels, magazines and photographs. With such limited references, often discovered by accident, period flower arranging is largely interpretative of the style, atmosphere, colours and characteristics of a period, rather than authentic reproductions of flower arrangements of the time.

Period Pieces for Today

As with any interpretative work, *all* the components of an exhibit/display should be made to play their part:

The plant material is the most important part – not only what is used, but how it is used. Modern hybrids are larger, showier and often in different colours from the long-ago versions. Choose for size, form and colour. Substitutes should be acceptable as long as the 'feel' is right, for example dahlias for peonies, single spray chrysanthemums for daisies, and modern spray carnations for old-fashioned pinks.

The style and shape of the arrangement may be quite different from present-day arrangements. A simple bunch may be called for or massed profusion; a garland or a tight rounded posy.

Authentic containers may not be possible, but much can be faked with plastic replicas, tins, stick-on decorations and spray paints.

Colours and colour combinations can indicate the period: the jewel colours of Tudor times, the pastels of the rococo style, the harsh aniline dyes of the Victorian period.

Bases, even if they were not used at the time, may be able to suggest the floor or the furniture on which flowers stood.

Backgrounds and fabrics can accentuate period atmosphere. Many modern wallpapers and fabrics can be adapted and used. Take care that the background does not become dominant, however interesting and appropriate it may be.

Accessories, even if authentic and exquisite, do not make a period piece out of a modern arrangement.

Lettering for titles, etc., should also be in period if possible.

The total composition of the display should convey the atmosphere of the period – classically simple or rather cluttered, balanced symmetrically or asymmetrically.

Mechanics

Generally speaking, modern mechanics like floral foam can be used because they are not seen once the arranging is done. But when the mechanics are visible, as in glass vases, then they should be of the period, for example moss or sand in Victorian times and the mesh covers of rose-bowls in the 1930s.

Researching

Research into a period and its style can be absorbing, but it is also time-consuming, and until the middle of the 19th century only a very few books (mostly unobtainable today) had been written about the way flowers were arranged. After about 1870 more information becomes available, much of it condensed into three reference books that will help present-day period arrangers. They are:

A History of Flower Arrangement by Julia S Berrall (Thames & Hudson, 1953, 1969, 1978 (softback)

A History of Flower Arranging edited by Dorothy Cooke & Pamela McNicol (Heinemann, 1989)

Guide to Period Flower Arranging (NAFAS, 1982, 1992)

This chapter deals with the flower arrangements of five different periods (Tudor, Georgian, Victorian, Edwardian and Art Deco), but there are many other historical eras or styles about which we know something of their ways with flowers. They include Ancient Egypt, Greece and Rome; the Byzantine empire; Renaissance Italy; 17th- and 18th-century Holland; rococo France; India; Persia; China; Japan; Colonial America.

A TUDOR TANKARD

The brilliant jewel colours of this simple bunch of flowers in a pewter tankard reflect the 16th century's love of bright mixed colours. All the flowers in the tankard were known to the Tudors, either growing in the wild or brought into their gardens for cultivation. The two most important were rosemary (Rosmarinus officinalis) and the 'gilly flowers'. Members of the dianthus family, gilly flowers included the garden pink (D. caryophyllus), sweet william (D. barbatus) and the larger border carnation usually called the 'coronation' in contemporary writings. The name 'gilly flower' is said to derive from either 'July flowers' or the French gilofre, meaning clove-scented.

OVERALL SIZE (W×H)
40 × 50 cm (16 × 20 in)

YOU WILL NEED
Pewter stemmed cup, mug or tankard (see method)
2 pewter (or pewter-finish) plates

PLANT MATERIAL
Mixture of spring and early-summer flowers including: pink (or spray carnation), daffodil, iris, tulip, primrose, snake's head fritillary, bluebell, hellebore, wallflower, grape hyacinth, rosemary and spurge (Euphorbia cyparissus)

For the plates: (right) apples, pears, grapes, walnuts, cherries; (left) rose-petal pot-pourri

Pomander: medium-sized orange thickly studded with 50 g (2 oz) cloves and decorated with narrow ribbons and pearl beads on pins

ARRANGER
Daphne Vagg

1 · A very good imitation of pewter can be achieved with kitchen foil and black shoe polish or matt black emulsion paint. It's easiest to start with an old plate with a flat rim. Cut a rough circle of foil about 2.5 cm (1 in) larger than the plate. Spread all-purpose clear adhesive over the face of the plate and press on the foil, Smoothing it out will leave wrinkles and creases, but these are needed. Turn the edges of the foil over to the underside. Cut a second circle rather smaller and do the same to the bottom of the plate. Brush the foil with black shoe polish or emulsion paint, pressing it into the creases. Rub it off before it dries, leaving black in the crevices. The same can be done with a mug or jug using separate pieces of foil for the handle. Joins will hardly show.

2 · Pick or buy as wide a variety as possible of the suggested flowers. Try to include bright red, pink, blue, yellow, mauve and white. Remember that perfume was as important as colour in those days of unwashed bodies and open sewers.

3 · It is probably easiest to arrange the flowers as a bunch in the hand, using the rosemary and taller flowers for height and mixing the colours like a jewel-box. Put the bunch into the tankard, three-quarters filled with water.

4 · Allow the flowers to settle and tuck in shorter flowers such as primroses, pansies and grape hyacinths around the container rim.

5 · Arrange the fruit on the plate. Pictured here is a group based on part of a painting of Lord Cobham and his family by Hans Eworth in 1567.

6 · The plate on the left holds pot-pourri and a pomander (which in Tudor time would have been worn on a loop over the wrist or tied to the waist).

Checking the Arrangement

The arrangement in the picture is standing on a small three-legged stool on a carpet laid over a table. Carpets were too precious to put on floors, which were usually strewn with rushes and the clippings of box or santolina from hedges in the knot gardens. Beside the tankard is a rushnip holding a rushlight made from the centre pith of a rush dipped in wax; in the 16th century this would have been animal tallow.

Other Options

Although spring and early summer are the most colourful periods for re-creating a Tudor-style arrangement, the atmosphere of the 16th century can be captured by bowls or pitchers of herbs that bloom later in summer. Angelica, chamomile, artemisia, asperula (sweet woodruff), balm, basil, borage, fennel, hyssop, lavender, marjoram, mint, parsley, sage, santolina, tansy and thyme were all grown and used for cooking and medicines.

Later summer flowers include the wild dog rose (*Rosa canina*), columbine (aquilegia), peonies, old-fashioned garden roses, lilies (especially *Lilium candidum*), bellflowers (campanula), anemones, double red ranunculus,

hollylocks, nasturiums, corn-flowers and honeysuckle. A posy or nosegay of any of these mixed with herbs would have been carried or placed in a room to freshen the air and ward off the plague.

At Christmas the evergreens, such as bay, box, cypress, fir, holly, ivy, myrtle, rosemary and yew, come into their own.

The 16th Century

Rich colour was much loved in Tudor times, and homes were more colourful than most people visualize, although we see echoes of it today in the restored painted ceilings of stately homes and chapels and in wall-hung tapestries. Indoors, if tapestries were too expensive, painted

cloths took their place. Outside, the plasterwork between beams was painted with orpiment (yellow), minium (burnt orange), cinnabar (brownish red), or rose madder (bright pink), all of which were of course earth pigments. Embroidery silks rejoiced in names like lady-blush, dove-coloured, pound-citron, marigold, brazil and watchet blue.

A Georgian Bough Pot

In Georgian times it was customary to arrange furniture against the walls, so the fireplace was always a dominant feature. To avoid leaving a gaping dark hole in the summer months when a fire was not needed, a 'bough' pot was often filled with flowers and foliage and placed on the hearth slab. In a contemporary cartoon of George III and his queen, flowers and leaves are arranged in a two-handled urn behind the grate bars. The inspiration for the arrangement here, however, has come from a conversation piece, 'The Vicar of the parish in the house of the infant squire', painted by Gawen Hamilton in the 18th century.

OVERALL SIZE (W × H)
100 × 75 cm (40 × 30 in)

YOU WILL NEED
A ceramic urn or a footed bowl (those with a flat back are true bough pots but are collectors' pieces today)

MECHANICS
Crumpled 5 cm (2 in) wire mesh
Wire or tape to secure it

PLANT MATERIAL
7–9 stems white larkspur
Blue periwinkle (Vinca major)
4–5 stems snowball tree (Viburnum opulus 'Sterile')
Stems of dill or Queen Anne's lace
5 white iris
5 yellow tulips
7 pink roses
5 Arum italicum leaves

ARRANGER
Anne Luckett

Fireplace decorations in summer were not uncommon even in 16th-century Britain but seem then to have been constructed from growing plants . The Georgians introduced cut flowers in containers.

1 · The arrangement is best done *in situ*, so that the height and width can be judged to cover the fire opening. Often, because the hearth is narrow, there is little depth for the arrangement yet it should not look too much like a flat cardboard cut-out.

2 · Tape or wire the crumpled mesh into the container, allowing it to dome up over the container rim. Floral foam can be used, of course, but it should not be higher than the container rim: 2.5 cm (1 in) or so lower is preferred, otherwise it is all too easy to have down-flowing stems, which were not possible at the time unless stems had a natural curve.

3 · The fan-shaped arrangement was popular in the 18th century. To establish a suitable outline put in seven larkspur stems at the back of the container – one vertical in the centre, one on each side almost horizontal and the others more or less equi-distant between. The aim is symmetry, but not with mathematical exactness.

4 · Keeping in mind that plant material should not actually come beyond the edge of the hearth, put in several arum leaves coming forward over the container rim and the periwinkle to the left.

5 · The snowball tree (viburnum) branches go in next, their stems softening the outline spikes.

6 · Fill in with the dill or Queen Anne's lace.

7 · The iris make a roughly diagonal line from top right to bottom left and the tulips run across the arrangement in an uneven horizontal line.

8 · The pink roses bring a bolder shape and slightly deeper colour towards the centre to focus interest, but notice that one is tucked at the back to take the colour through and give a greater feeling of depth.

Checking the Arrangement

The colours chosen here are pastels and whites, toning in with the white-painted woodwork and green marble surround. The Georgians liked their colours clear or pastel, but not gaudy. The effect to aim at is one of quality and refined taste.

Other Options

There is not space here to list all the flowers that were available in Georgian times but many were grown for the grander homes in hot-houses and cutting gardens. They included the carnation and pink, lily, rose, lilac, peony, antirrhinum, tuberose, auricula, anemone, hyacinth and narcissus.

In winter-time, of course, the fire would have been lit, but as we nowadays have other forms of heating, a bough pot of dried flowers and grasses would be very suitable, especially those which are commonly grown in gardens today.

Other Georgian-style containers used on tables, chests and commodes included many shapes of urns in both china and metal, flower bricks and vases with perforated tops, five-fingered posy holders, Chinese export porcelain bowls and vases, and those made by the famous 18th century porcelain factories of Chelsea, Bow, Rockingham, Derby and Staffordshire.

The 18th Century

This was the era of Lancelot 'Capability' Brown, the English landscape gardener who introduced the highly picturesque 'natural look' to the parklands of the nation's stately homes. Graceful, well-proportioned arrangements like this one suited the period's elegant interiors, newly flooded with light from the tall windows that had become fashionable.

A VICTORIAN DINING TABLE

OVERALL SIZE

The table is 223 × 122 cm (88 × 48 in); the tallest arrangement is 90 cm (36 in) high and the two lower ones about 60 cm (24 in) high

YOU WILL NEED

1 tall and 2 shorter three-tiered stands, painted gold and the containers decorated with gold fringe

Soaked floral foam

For each swag: 2 stub wires, white stem binding tape, cellophane tape, 40 cm (16 in) white waterproof ribbon 5 cm (2 in) wide, piece of soaked floral foam, cling film, sticky tape, heavy glass ashtray, or weighted tin painted white (see photo)

Scallop shells painted white with gold edges, two for each swag and groups of three as sweetmeat dishes

PLANT MATERIAL

5 × 150 cm (60 in) trails of smilax (Asparagus medeoloides) (trails of ivy are an alternative)

Asparagus ferns (A. plumos and A. sprengeri), davallia and maidenhair ferns, rhamnus, euonymus, cupressus, ivy and similar foliage

For one swag and the centre stand (adjust amounts for the smaller stands):

10 purple hanging bracts of Leycesteria formosa

10 stems each carnations and spray carnations in 3 shades of pink

4 stems spray chrysanthemums in yellow and pink

4 stems golden rod

10 stems cluster roses

3 stems cream lilies

12 purple physostegia

1 stem September flower/gypsophila

ARRANGER

Margot Camp

Table decorations of flowers date only from the mid-19th century, when it became fashionable to dine à la Russe, *with the servants handing around and later removing each course in turn. Up to that time it had been customary for all the dishes to be set out at the beginning of a meal and allowed to accumulate until the dessert course. Then everything was cleared away and the cloth was 'drawn', revealing either the bare polished table, or another cloth beneath. With the advent of dining* à la Russe *the cloth remained in place throughout the meal and hostesses soon began to vie with each other to impress their guests with more and more elaborate floral decorations.*

1 · Fit each stand with soaked foam in each of its containers to protrude above the rim by 2.5 cm (1 in). Where the rod comes in the centre, shape the foam to fit in two halves. There is no need to tape it in if it fits firmly, as this would restrict the space for stems.

2 · If two side stands are being arranged, divide the flowers and foliage equally before you start. Begin by arranging the trailing ferns and drops of leycesteria. Use other foliage to start covering the mechanics and to establish the width and length of the arrangement in the lowest container. It can be round or oval to suit the rest of the table.

3 · In the two top containers the flowers will be fairly short-stemmed and in tight posies, but the lower arrangement can be more spreading. Use the larger lily flowers and single carnations in the lower one, keeping the smaller flowers for the very top.

4 · Now make the swags. First divide the flowers and foliage equally – they must look matched, if not exactly so. For each swag cover two 38 cm (15 in) stub wires with white stem-binding tape. Fix them with cellophane tape to the back of the length of white waterproof ribbon. Cut a 'V' into one end of the ribbon; this is the top. Turn the ribbon over. Wrap a piece of soaked foam 10×5×4 cm (4×2×1½ in) in cling film and tape it firmly with two bands of sticky tape to the ribbon about 10 cm (4 in) from the straight end. Put a piece of wet foam in the ashray to protrude about 2.5 cm (1 in) above the rim.

5 · Insert foliage and flowers into the taped-on piece of foam to cover the bottom end of the ribbon and to come 5 cm (2 in) towards the top. Arrange a posy in the glass dish.

6 · Now take both to the table. Bend the ribbon and its wire about 5 cm (2 in) above the foam block to make a right angle. Lay the V-end piece on the table and weight it down with the glass dish. The weight is essential. Finish off the two arrangements so that they look as one.

7 · Two scallop shells were arranged fan-wise on the table to finish it off at the back. A ribbon bow would also be possible.

8 · The smilax is added last, swagged in curves from one posy to the next. Insert the stem ends into the foam in one dish and then trim the other end to tuck in the next dish.

Checking the Arrangement

● Candlesticks or candelabra, starched napkins folded in fantastic shapes, menu holders, place names and posies for the ladies can all be added. The Victorians liked the effect to be heavy and overdone, and you may well wonder how room was found for food, place settings and glasses–and how you sat down to such a table in a crinoline!

● The table is covered and draped to the floor with cream fabric overlaid with white nylon curtaining. The Victorians would have used starched white damask.

Other Options

According to the size of the table, the number of stands and swags needed will vary and heights may be altered. Three stands were used here. They do take a great deal of plant material and must be planned to suit the budget.

While ivy or jasmine can be substituted for smilax, some ferns are needed in the stands for a true Victorian feel. Flowers may be any of the old-fashioned types at any time of year, such as pansies, fuchsias, hyacinths, sweet williams, antirrhinums.

The 19th Century

The Victorian love of excess showed itself in prodigious ornamentation and heavy use of pattern and colour. The period saw the revival of many historical styles, particularly the Gothic and Greek Revivals, in what became know as the 'battle of the styles'. Japanese-style decoration and exotic imports from the East were also popular, as well as orchids, palms and other hothouse plants which were brought back from the tropics by the Victorian missionaries and botanists.

AN EDWARDIAN FIREPLACE

The Edwardian treatment of the fireplace and hearth when not in use in summer was very different from the Georgian. In the early part of the 20th century the emphasis was more on the use of houseplants than actual arrangements of cut flowers, but a combination of the two could produce a lavish display. In many homes of the time it was the gardener's job to 'furnish the fireplace' from the garden or greenhouse. Today there is a wide choice of houseplants for the flower arranger.

OVERALL SIZE (W × H)
168 × 137 cm (66 × 54 in)

YOU WILL NEED
2 wooden stands or boxes to make different heights, matt black fabric to cover
1 large ceramic or brass pot
2–3 small containers

MECHANICS
Soaked floral foam for main and subsidiary containers

PLANT MATERIAL
Tall variegated Ficus benjamina
*Palm (*Chamaedorea elegans*)*
4 flowering Begonia elatior
2 small kalanchoë
Ferns: nephrolepis, bird's nest, maidenhair
Solanum, dieffenbachia
2 'Enchantment' lilies
Philodendron scandens
Cut flowers and foliage:
5 stems berried pyracantha
12 dried blue hydrangea heads
3 stems ming fern
7–8 clusters hydrangea autumn foliage
10 yellow roses
6 stems longiflorum lilies
3 stems gold spray chrysanthemums

ARRANGER
Mary Gwyther

1 · Leave the plants in their pots. Occasionally it may be necessary (because the pot will not fit into a small awkward space) to remove one from its pot and put it into a polythene bag.

2 · Arrange the stands/boxes to create two levels above the hearth. Drape with fabric (omitted from first photo to make the construction clearer). Position the tallest plants on each side first, on the top level. Here the *Ficus benjamina* is on the left, and the palm on the right. Put the large bowl or pot in the centre of the hearth with blocks of soaked foam ready to take cut flowers and foliage.

3 · Group the bird's nest and nephrolepis ferns and smaller plants on either side and the maidenhair fern behind the fender. Tuck the dried hydrangea heads behind and below the nephrolepis fern and balance the blue colour with two or three behind the central pot and tucked down by the maidenhair fern.

4 · The pyracantha and pots of orange lilies are in a container on the top level on the right, and help cover the large pot behind.

5 · Arrange the stems of Ming fern, the hydrangea foliage and the yellow roses loosely in the centre container.

6 · Add the longiflorum lilies, allowing the trumpets to curve down right to the fender.

7 · Gold spray chrysanthemums are cut short and put into soaked foam in a small container to cover the flowerpot of the smooth-leaved fern, and a dieffenbachia finishes off the grouping at floor level on the left.

8 · A few ivy trails based in soaked foam in a small container and the philodendron on the mantelpiece complete the display.

Checking the Arrangement

● Aim to have three different levels: the hearth itself, then two more levels, each about 18–20 cm (7–8 in) higher. In the picture which follows step 2, you can see the rough step constructions used here.
● The steps were draped with black fabric. If the fireplace is not

black, the colour could be dull pine green or a colour to tone with the fireplace tiling. The draping may not be needed if plants will obscure all the staging.

Other Options

Almost any houseplants and cut flowers can be assembled for these groupings, but try to include some ferns, which are so typical. Ivy or other climbers can be taken up over a mirror or picture hanging above the mantelpiece.

The Early 20th Century

In spite of the heavily decorated hearth, most arrangements in Edwardian times were lighter, with more space in them, than the Victorians' flowers.

Japanese anemones, dahlias, day lilies, martagon and auratum lilies, spirea, chrysanthemums, michaelmas daisies, asters, fennel, poppies and other hardy border flowers made their appearance in the Edwardian era, along with grasses and gypsophila.

Photographs of the garden designer Gertrude Jekyll's own decorations often show two associated flower arrangements in a tall vase and a low bowl beside it, and still-life groups of fruit with pewter vases or jugs.

King Edward VII's favourite flowers were said to be sweet peas. Prettily arranged in low epergnes with silver or silver-plated trumpets (instead of the tall glass trumpets of the Victorians), with asparagus and maidenhair ferns or gypsophila, they adorned hundreds of dinner tables.

ART DECO

Although the style known as Art Deco was affecting the design of architecture, furniture, fabrics, ceramics, lighting and ornaments during the 1930s, its geometric lines seem to have had little influence on the flower arrangements of the time. These were, in the main, simple and naturalistic, with the emphasis on garden and wild flowers reflecting the great upsurge of interest in suburban gardening and home decoration. So for exhibition and 'period' flower pieces, the style of the era is often interpreted rather than re-creations of the actual arrangements.

OVERALL SIZE (W × H)
66 × 100 cm (26 × 39 in)

YOU WILL NEED
2 blocks or boxes
Black felt to cover
Round black dish
Split-cane fan
2 Art deco pieces – used here are a pewter figurine and a Clarice Cliff covered dish

MECHANICS
Piece of soaked floral foam
Sticky tape
Green garden canes
Putty-type adhesive
Silver rose wires

PLANT MATERIAL
Nasturtiums and leaves

ARRANGER
Colette Archer

1 · Cover the blocks or boxes neatly with black felt to act as plinths for the figurine and the container. Tape the foam into the dish and place it centrally on one of the plinths.

2 · The two fan shapes (representing the sun-ray shape so popular with Art Deco designers) are cut from one large imported fan and the two parts mounted, with tape, on to garden canes.

3 · The large fan is fixed in the back of the foam with the point almost resting on it. The small fan is in the centre on a longer cane. Although the finished arrangement is balanced asymmetrically, the fans are central and symmetrical.

4 · Before arranging the flowers, position the figurine on the other block and the vegetable dish on the right of the base.

5 · A long trail of nasturtium establishes the main line from the top of the fan almost down to the base.

6 · A second stem, at the top, can be carefully wired to the fans in one or two places to keep it in position. The wires can be hidden by flowers or leaves.

7 · Add more sprays and single flowers or leaves so the orange and green colours make a curving natural line. Adjust the positions of the two accessories if necessary.

Checking the Arrangement

● The arranger has managed to combine several Art Deco features – the figurine and pottery dish, the sunray shape, the colour scheme, the general impression – with the naturalistic style of flower arrangement of the time.
● Orange is perhaps the colour most typical of the 1930s, and the brilliance of nasturtiums and their easy growth from seed made them extremely popular flowers. Their shape and that of the leaves is echoed in Clarice Cliff pottery.

Other Options

The orange colour could have been emphasized equally well by pot marigolds (calendula), Chinese lanterns (Cape gooseberries or physalis) or the brilliant orange seeds of the stinker iris (*Iris foetidissima*).

The 1930s

At this time flower arrangements for the home began to be featured in magazines and talks on the radio. Anne Lamplugh was one of the broadcasters and she published two books, *Flower and Vase* (1929) and *My Flower Decoration Notebook* (1937), subtitled 'the weekly diary of an ordinary woman's flower arrangements'.

In 1934 Constance Spry, perhaps the best-known of all flower arrangers, published her first book, *Flower Decoration*, which was to be followed by many others. Her shop in the West End of London provided flowers for the well-to-do in a loose, flowing style that was described as 'billowing and lavish'.

Constance Spry's hallmark was to use all kinds of plant materials together for decorative effect. Lichened branches were grouped with cabbage leaves, hedgerow berries with hothouse lilies, green leaves alone with no flowers, and green and white arrangements, which were special favourites.

Her dream was that everyone, not just the rich, should enjoy flowers in their home. To this end she gave talks to gardening and women's groups all over the world and later encouraged the formation of flower clubs and judged their shows.

Yet, curiously, enough, neither Anne Lamplugh nor Constance Spry seems to have been affected by the Art Deco style that was so ubiquitous, even in very modest homes, in the 1930s.

CHAPTER NINE · REVIEW

*P*eriod flowers arrangements are often needed for historical displays and stately homes. Interpreting the style, atmosphere, colours and characteristics of a historical period using flowers, containers and mechanics available today can re-create the atmosphere of the time very successfully, though total accuracy is often impracticable. The analysis given here will help to make the details as authentic as possible.

Period Flower Arrangements

16TH & 17TH CENTURIES: TUDOR, STUART

CONTAINERS	FOLIAGE	FLOWERS ETC	COLOURS	SETTINGS	STYLE
Pewter tankards, jugs and bowls	Bay, yew, box rosemary, broom, herbs	Gillyflowers (use pinks, sweet williams, stocks), carnation, rose, pansy, primrose, iris	Polychromatic: primaries and bright jewel colours	Beam and plaster walls	Simple bunches
Treen				Linenfold panelling	Tussie-mussies
Clear glass decanter shapes				Tapestries and painted cloths	Nosegays of herbs and sweet-smelling flowers
Blackjacks in leather		Apples, pears, grapes, walnuts		Oak and elm woods	'Crown' garlands (on head)
					Pot-pourri
					Pomanders

18TH CENTURY: GEORGIAN

CONTAINERS	FOLIAGE	FLOWERS ETC	COLOURS	SETTINGS	STYLE
Bough pots	Oak, beech, magnolia, privet, rosemary	Hot house: lily, carnation	Mixed pastels: grey-green, pale blue, rose-pink, pale coffee and white	Elegant rooms, well-proportioned doors and windows	Fan-shaped arrangements
Urns – porcelain and metal		Peony, rose, lilac, delphinium		Striped and toile de Jouy fabrics	Rounded outlines
Chinese export vases		Oranges, pineapples, peaches, apricots	Gold/ormolu/ gilding	Walnut, satinwood	Bough-pots in hearths
Flower bricks					
Five-finger posyholders					

19TH CENTURY: VICTORIAN

CONTAINERS	FOLIAGE	FLOWERS ETC	COLOURS	SETTINGS	STYLE
Tall epergnes with glass trumpets *March stands* *Narrow-necked vases* *Posy holders (to carry)* *Tall glass trumpet vases* *Curious shapes: boot, hand, swan, shell*	*Ferns: Asparagus (A. plumosus and A. Spregerii), smilax, maidenhair* *Ivy, aspidistra, laurel, parlour palms*	*Rose, pansy, lily, phlox, tuberose, fuchsia, pink, mignonette, calceolaria* *Pampas grass*	*First aniline dyes: magenta, grassy green, wine red, brown, black, 'carnation' pink* *Touch of yellow 'to bring all alive'*	*Flocked wallpapers* *Velvets, damask, plush* *Fringes, tassels and bobbles* *Lace curtains* *Mahogany and rosewood*	*Posies: to carry, on dresses, hair, bosoms, petticoats – everywhere* *Over-elaborate table flowers, with trailing ferns and patterns of leaves* *Vases, dotted about rooms*

20TH CENTURY: EDWARDIAN

CONTAINERS	FOLIAGE	FLOWERS ETC	COLOURS	SETTINGS	STYLE
'Ellen Terry' stands *Indian brass trays, bowls and vases* *Pewter and copper utensils* *Cut glass bowls and vases* *Low epergnes with silver or plated trumpets*	*Asparagus fern* *Grey-leaved plants* *Beech* *Foliage from flowering shrubs*	*Carnation, lily, sweet pea, rose, gypsophila, poppy, tulip, delphinium, chrysanthemum, honeysuckle, fruit blossom* *Honesty seedheads*	*Beige, grey, mauve, apricot, eau-de-nil, silver, black and white, blue (including navy)*	*Cream and white painted woodwork* *Art Nouveau and William Morris influenced interiors* *White marble or tiled fireplaces* *Mahogany, limed oak, walnut, satinwood*	*Tall vases with simple, tall arrangements* *Elaborate table decorations* *Plants and vases of flowers in hearths*

20TH CENTURY: THE INTER-WAR YEARS

CONTAINERS	FOLIAGE	FLOWERS ETC	COLOURS	SETTINGS	STYLE
Cut glass *Coloured frosted glass* *Ceramic posy rings* *Unglazed terracotta pitchers* *Fretted rose bowls* *Clarice Cliff and Susie Cooper pottery*	*Green and copper beech* *Hosta, bergenia* *Horse-chestnut buds*	*Marigold, nasturtium, Chinese lanterns, (physalis) geranium, dahlia, michaelmas daisy, China aster, mimosa, daffodil, anenome, chrysanthemum* *Pussy willow*	*Orange, blue, jade green, red, yellow, glossy black, chrome silver, rust*	*Beige, oatmeal or flower-patterned walls* *Chromium furniture* *Black shiny surfaces* *Geometric patterns* *Limed, light & dark oak*	*Loose, spreading arrangements* *Forced blossom in tall jugs* *Small 'landscapes' and dish gardens* *Low bowls of floating flowers*

Chapter Ten

ON A LARGER
SCALE

*As a flower arranger becomes more experienced it is likely that he or
she will be asked to undertake, or be one of a team to undertake,
a larger-scale flower arranging display. It may be the flower club
exhibit in a local competitive show, an interpretative display for the church
festival or something to enliven a dark corner in a stately home.
Never turn down such an invitation. It is a wonderful experience in
every way and certainly not one to be missed.*

*W*orking *as a* team is very different from working alone or even with just a helper, but be assured there will always be help and advice at hand, and if you are sensible you will take it. Working with new people in fascinating settings is an opportunity from which you are bound to benefit.

Working as a Team

When you are working as a team, there must be give-and-take in thinking of ideas, doing the research and sharing the workload (including the less interesting chores). It may also involve sharing the expenses, though these are generally met, at least to a certain limit, by the club or organizers of the event.

An ideal flower arrangement team for a really large exhibit is three. There should be one experienced arranger with some flair and designing ability. Another needs to be reliable and practical, with plenty of commonsense and the ability to work with others and to see all sides of a problem. The third should be keen, up-and-coming but perhaps not yet with much experience; this person will make the lists and the coffee, soak the foam, paint the containers and be a general dogsbody while he/she learns the ropes. Not many teams are as ideally balanced, but something like this should be the aim.

Qualities apart, personalities must be able to work together. Either the first or second member will be the leader, whose authority to have the final say must be recognized by the other two, however much give-and-take there is.

In less demanding circumstances a pair of arrangers, often friends or at least two people who live near each other, can work together as a team.

Where one arranger is able to accomplish all the flower arranging it is still sensible, when working on a large exhibit, to have a helper. This person may not even be a flower arranger, but he/she can help by driving, parking the car, carrying in some of the props, bucketing the flowers, holding the steps, fetching water and packing up the rubbish.

A team will need to meet once or twice at the planning stage, especially if research into the title has to be done and props borrowed or made.

Mock-ups

At least two mock-ups will be needed, possibly more, in a space carefully marked out according to the schedule or brief given.

In a competitive show this is most important, for if the space allowed is exceeded, disqualification will follow and all the hard work will have been for nothing. In a festival or exhibition it is equally important, because if the designers have asked for something 270 cm (9 ft) high × 150 cm (5 ft) wide, they will not be pleased to get something larger – or smaller.

Never guess what a measurement looks like. Mark it out accurately with chalk, string or tapes, so that it is exact. Distances are always deceptive, and what looked huge at home will suddenly look very small and insignificant in a church or great exhibition hall.

Height

Working out how to get and support the necessary height is often one of the most difficult parts of planning a large exhibit. This can be achieved in various ways, depending, of course, on the theme proposed.

Driftwood is often used with several pieces bolted and screwed together (a handyman can be a great help). It may be self-supporting or fixed to a metal or hardboard base, which will have other weight on it for stability (see pages 94–5, 126–7 and 156–7). It has the great advantage that it is natural plant material so there is no problem if it should dominate the exhibit.

A telescopic metal rod that screws into a metal base can be a useful long-term buy from a blacksmith. Bamboo poles, stems of dried giant hogweed or polygonum, wooden or plastic crates, small pieces of furniture piled up, carpet rolls or plastic piping (from do-it-yourself stores) made into pillars (see page 158) by painting or spraying to look like stone, marble or metal, can all be used.

Draped fabrics are useful to obscure supports and to link different parts of the exhibit, but must be used with discretion or they become dominant and overwhelm the flowers.

The following pages examine in detail six large-scale arrangements with different constructions and for different purposes.

TALL CHURCH COLUMN

A column of flowers, often much taller than a person, is a popular decoration for special festivals and weddings in church. The very solidity of this column makes it showy in large and spacious surroundings. But it does take a lot of flowers: almost 180 quite large ones were used here. It can easily be done by one arranger but a helper to hand up stems for the higher placements saves a lot of climbing up and down. This becomes an exercise in the teamwork that larger arrangements often need.

OVERALL SIZE (W × H)
75 × 215 cm (30 × 85 in)

YOU WILL NEED
Stout wood stand with three shelves
Small pair of steps

MECHANICS
4 plastic margarine or ice-cream boxes
4 blocks soaked floral foam
Green sticky tape
Green paint or spray

PLANT MATERIAL
3 bunches leather fern
20 stems alchemilla
35 stems cream delphiniums
40 stems cream astilbe
18 pink lilies
25 pink carnations
18 cream gerberas
Fillers: sprays of weigela and green beech, bergenia and hosta leaves

ARRANGER
Mary Bultitude

Once the stand has been constructed it can be used over and over again. Only the floral foam has to be replaced.

1 · The stand can easily be made from a 168 cm (66 in) length of 5 × 5 cm (2 × 2 in) wood screwed to a wooden base about 45 × 30 cm (18 × 12 in). Three small shelves about 10 cm (4 in) deep and about 15 cm (6 in) wide are fixed with right-angle brackets to the pole. The first is 64 cm (25 in) from the base, the next is 50 cm (20 in) above the first, and the last is at the top. Although the upright here has been bound with waterproof ribbon to make a decorative finish, it is often sensible to paint the whole stand a dark green or black so that when the arrangement is completed, the support itself is scarcely seen.

2 · Four plastic ice-cream or margarine boxes are painted or sprayed green, filled with soaked foam that protrudes 5 cm (2 in) and then taped firmly to each shelf with crossing bands of green sticky tape. It helps to have the bottom box a little larger than the others to give more weight and stability. Steps will be needed to reach the top shelf. Use a proper step-ladder; don't try to reach by standing on a chair.

3 · Start by creating roughly triangular outlines on each shelf with the leather fern, other

foliages and some alchemilla. The base arrangement should be widest, the next shelf up a little narrower and so on.

4 · Cream delphiniums follow the outlines and make the framework larger. The final height is established with a tall stem. This is where another pair of hands is helpful, either to hand up what is requested, or, from a more experienced helper, to anticipate what may be needed next.

5 · Hosta and bergenia leaves are added to cover the mechanics and the shelves.

6 · Astilbe, lilies and carnations are distributed fairly evenly through the stand, gradually building up the four separate arrangements into a tapering column of flowers and foliage which has no discernible breaks. Use any remaining foliage to fill in gaps.

7 · Finally, the pink gerberas, the largest and most eye-catching flowers, are taken down through the column in a series of sweeping S-curves to give rhythm to the whole structure.

8 · Before leaving, make sure all boxes are topped up with water and, if possible, mist-spray the whole arrangement if it can be done without damage to the surrounding pillars, woodwork, hangings, carvings or carpet.

Checking the Arrangement

● When completed, the column should not show where the different sections join.
● Check the length of stems to ensure a gradual tapering towards the top.

Other Options

For a wedding or at Easter-time or Harvest Festival the large amount of flowers used here may not seem extravagant, but at other times similar columns can be created with foliage, Queen Anne's lace or dried and glycerined materials. At Harvest time the inclusion of fruit and vegetables can be very impressive. They can also be piled nearby at the base. A cascading effect can be achieved by using ivy trails, garden clematis or wild clematis (known as 'old man's beard'), rambler roses, asparagus fern or jasmine.

A pair of columns like this looks good flanking entrance doors or archways or on either side of an altar.

FLOOR PARALLELS

The parallel style, shown as a smaller arrangement on page 23, is equally effective on a larger and bolder scale in churches, halls and theatres. Carried out in vivid colours, as here, the effect is stunning. There is a lot of detailed work to be done to create the packed groundwork, but it is possible (if necessary) to do this in advance, leaving the taller placements to be arranged in situ. The tall spires echo the strong verticals of much church architecture.

OVERALL SIZE (W ×H)
200 × 120 cm (78 × 48 in)

YOU WILL NEED
9 raffia-covered long, narrow baskets (or plant troughs) in three different sizes
9 shallow plastic trays (to use as liners if basket used)
Metal stand or wooden frame to raise one larger container

MECHANICS
16 blocks soaked floral foam

PLANT MATERIAL
10 mauve delphiniums
12 purple liatris
12 purple alliums
15 orange lilies
3 white delphiniums
2 bunches white sweet peas
10 white carnations
9 green molucellas
10 orange carnations
10 orange roses
6 sprays cerise orchids
6 orange gerberas
4 large oranges, 3 yellow peppers
Fillers: alchemilla, Asparagus sprengeri, hosta and mahonia leaves

ARRANGER
Tom Hodge

1 · Place the soaked blocks of foam in all containers. You will need 1½–2 for each of the larger ones. They should protrude above the containers by at least 2.5 cm (1 in). One large basket/trough is raised about 45 cm (18 in) at the back of the others, which are arranged in a staggered row.

2 · Start on the left with a column of mauve delphiniums arranged in both the raised and lower troughs. Repeat a shorter column about three-quarters of the way along to the right.

3 · Between the two, about midway, put a column of purple liatris and next to it a graded vertical of six purple allium heads, more or less equally spaced in height. On the extreme right set a line of three allium heads less than half the height of the other. This establishes the main placements in purple colouring.

4 · Next, put in the four blocks of orange lilies, in tight groups of varying heights.

5 · White is a very eye-catching colour and is best dealt with at this stage. The column of white delphiniums is almost in the centre, with a bunch of white sweet peas clustered at the base of each group of mauve

delphiniums and a tight mass of white carnations at the foot of the tallest purple alliums.

6 · The green accents are mainly molucella spires and groups of green leaves at the lowest level to fill in the gaps and give weight near the container rims.

7 · Now the groundwork, or 'tapestry' as it is sometimes picturesquely called, needs to be filled in. Areas of very short-stemmed carnations, roses and orchids are used.

8 · The bold, round-faced orange gerberas make accent points in three places, and oranges and yellow peppers add different shapes and textures.

Checking the Arrangement

● It is possible, if time *in situ* is limited, to pre-arrange the shorter items in each container. To do this effectively it is necessary to have a fairly detailed plan of the arrangement of colour and flower blocks before starting. Most arrangers like to start with one or two of the taller groupings, spacing out the colours and adjusting the relative heights as they go.

● This type of parallel decoration is very versatile indeed as the units can be moved around quite easily. The smaller picture shows the effect achieved casually as the baskets were carried outside the church and put on the steps to be loaded into the van.

● For a large parallel decoration it is important to have the tall vertical placements bold enough to balance the considerable amount of plant material at the base. The bulky delphiniums, bunched liatris and allium heads are ideal for this. Straight stems are necessary, and if they are thin, flowers can be bunched or bundled (with their ties or cross

gartering shown decoratively) to give the needed bulk.

● In much the same way when making the solid base patchwork, the individual blocks of colour need to be bright enough and large enough to balance the tall verticals.

● The long plastic troughs for window sills or patios which can be bought from garden centres make good containers for parallel decorations, but may need disguising to suit their setting. Paint mixed with sand gives a better texture than the smooth plastic. Mottling with two or three different-coloured car sprays is effective. Pieces of bark or sections of dried stems can be glued on, to relieve the plainness, as can string patterns, pasta shapes, cords or cardboard cut into abstract shapes to give a textured look.

Other Options

This decoration was arranged in mid-summer but it can be equally effective in spring with daffodils, tulips, iris and smaller spring flowers at the base. In autumn, driftwood, bundles of corn or stripped ivy may provide verticals offset by fruits and vegetables at the bottom. At Christmas firs, yew and rosemary can stand above holly, poinsettias, carnations, fruit and nuts.

MASS LINE

It was the Italian arrangers who popularized the composite mass-line design using a large, heavy container to support plant materials that were both boldly linear and solidly massed. The design shown opposite could simply be a decorative sculpture, or with the title 'Temptation in the Garden' could become a strongly interpretative piece abstracting the essence of the story of Adam and Eve in the Garden of Eden.

OVERALL SIZE (W × H)
90 × 180 cm (36 × 72 in)

THE ARRANGER USED
Large heavy pot at least 55 cm (22 in) high

MECHANICS
Metal or wood rod to stand in pot to support a shallow tray or saucer on top to hold damp foam
Block of floral foam to fit
Green sticky tape
Kebab sticks

PLANT MATERIAL
2 clipped palm leaves on long stems
Tangle of clematis or other vine
Curves of vine to make circular shape
Branch or stripped ivy to resemble serpent
4 fatsia leaves
9 angelica heads
9 green apples

ARRANGER
John Wareing

1 · Clip the palm leaves into roughly diamond shapes.

2 · Wedge the palm stalks firmly into the pot and then add the supporting pole for the soaked foam which should be firmly taped to the saucer or tray.

3 · Position the tangle of vine over the top-right of the palm leaves and intertwine the branch or ivy to hang down on the right.

4 · Add the large loop of vine to the left of the pot. In size it should echo that of the tangle above; and, with its enclosed void, it should balance the group of leaves on the right.

5 · Place the fatsia leaves on the right of the foam block. Their large, shiny surfaces will contrast with the rough angelica heads (step 7).

6 · Seven green apples mounted on kebab sticks are clustered on the left in a bold group.

7 · Add the angelica heads in a central cluster, with the tallest coming about halfway up the palm stems. One head should come down over the pot rim on the right and one is tucked into the tangled mass above.

8 · Two smooth pebbles and two apples draw the eye down to the floor placement.

Checking the Arrangement

● As a large decorative piece this is an exciting study in asymmetrical balance and the clever contrasting of solids with spaces. The colour and textural balance is also well chosen. The circular forms are carefully repeated and contrasted: matt, rough angelica heads with smooth shiny apples, and the tangled vine mass with the empty wreath circle.

● As an interpretative design it is interesting to see how the arranger has chosen plant material to tell the story. The green garden flourishes in the centre, but the tempting apples are already there, and so are the fig leaves (represented by fatsia leaves) which will be used to cover Adam and Eve's shame as their downfall is accomplished by the serpent (branch) writhing down out of the tree. The tangle above may suggest chaos, which is bringing the world (one green angelica head) into being and so combines the scientific explanation of genesis with the Bible story. Each viewer will put his or her own interpretation on the arrangement, but the pointers are clearly chosen for their symbolic value: the apples, fig leaves and serpent will be recognized by most of us.

● British freestyle and abstract arranging generally tended to emphasize line and space, using form (perhaps just two or three flowers) in only a limited way as

eye-catching or accent points of colour. Continental arrangers, and the Italians in particular, demonstrated the value of massing flowers together (to them 20 massed carnations is nothing) to create very much larger and bolder areas of focus. But the

contrasting linear and spatial features are never overlooked. As seen in this picture, a circular void and a complicated mass of lines and spaces in the tangled clematis balance another space created by the downward line of the 'serpent'.

Other Options

A strongly personal interpretation like this can hardly be translated into other plant materials. But the thinking behind it can give many ideas, both for design and for interpretation.

TELLING A STORY

Festivals in stately homes and churches often require a large-scale exhibit to interpret a historical event, a Bible text, a quotation or some feature connected with the building, its interior or its purpose. The arranger here was asked to interpret 'The Resurrection' on a site that would be seen from virtually all sides towards the end of a long corridor. One could not repeat this display exactly, but it is interesting to see how she went about it.

OVERALL SIZE (W × D × H)
140 × 178 × 190 cm (55 × 70 × 75 in)

THE ARRANGER USED
2 large hardboard bases painted grey

2 pieces of driftwood to make an arch

1 long curving piece of stripped ivy for the top placement

4 other pieces of driftwood

MECHANICS
Blocks to raise one base

Custom-made metal rod on stand to support the ivy

4 shallow plastic trays

4 blocks soaked floral foam

Wire mesh

Gold spray paint

ACCESSORY
Length of white muslin

PLANT MATERIAL
8 gilded cycas ferns

3 gilded clipped palmetto fans

10 longiflorum lilies

Florist's and garden flowers: delphiniums, aconitum, iris, spiraea, roses, gypsophila, clematis, spray chrysanthemums, bergenia leaves, moss pads

ARRANGER
Margaret Whittaker

1 · The bases and the stand for the top placement are set up first. The driftwood is next assembled, propped and anchored as necessary and the long piece of stripped ivy wood is then secured to the stand.

2 · Three trays with one whole block each of soaked foam held on large 'frogs' are placed in position on the base, one in the front, one on the right and one at the back left. The tray on the top holds a full block of soaked foam, covered with paper and wire mesh (it needs extra support to hold long and heavy stems), all sprayed gold. Moss is laid over part of the base and a few leaves put in to start covering the mechanics.

3 · The top arrangement has to be done first, with the cycas ferns and palm fans spreading wide, like wings, to give the sense of resurrection and rising up. The lilies represent the purity and majesty of the risen Lord.

4 · The white draped 'winding sheet' (hiding the supporting rod) falls from the rising spirit down through the arched wood, now seen as the tomb from which the Lord has risen.

5 · Meanwhile, a garden has been created at the entrance to the rocky tomb, and behind it, with a mass of multi-coloured flowers amid the rocks. The predominant colours are pink and blue with some stronger crimson, but touches of white link with the colour of the fabric and the white lilies above.

Checking the Arrangement

● It is interesting that the garden is a very European one, making no attempt to evoke the landscape or Gethsemane garden of the Holy Land. It leaves the viewer wondering if this is a deliberate reminder that Christ's resurrection has a timeless and worldwide significance. All really

accessory. Does it add to the story portrayed? The answer is surely a clear 'yes', with the added fact that it significantly helps the design in linking the upper and lower placements. This could not have been so easily or effectively achieved with plant materials.

● This large all-round display posed problems for the photographer, as the camera could only see it from one static position, whereas viewers would be able to walk around at least three sides with changing viewpoints. The camera also found the stained glass window obtrusive and confusing to the top important placement. The viewer, on the other hand, would scarcely be aware of the window while looking at the exhibit. In all these large-scale groupings it is important to remember that pictures can only show a two-dimensional image of a three-dimensional form and the valued elements of space and depth are therefore missing here.

Other Options

There is never a right or wrong way to interpret a title, quotation or event. 'The Resurrection', if it were a class at a show, might produce a dozen different approaches to the title, and all would vary in detail and use different plant material. What matters is that the story should be portrayed clearly enough to be understood by everyone.

Another approach might be to construct a towering column (see pages 150–1) of white flowers, especially lilies, to suggest the Ascension. The Easter colours of gold, yellow and white would be the first choice of many arrangers for their liturgical symbolism.

For the flower arranger, it is important to remember that it should be the plant materials, not the accessories which really tell the story.

good interpretative designs do offer the viewer the opportunity to add his or her own interpretation to some aspects of the story being told. It should invite

involvement, just as a painting or sculpture does.

● The story is told here almost entirely in plant material, with the white fabric as the only

EVOLVING IMAGES

One of the club classes at the NAFAS 1992 Competitions at Glasgow had the title 'Evolving Images' with the quotation 'Each age is a dream that is dying or one that is coming to birth'. Further, it was to be 'an exhibit in period style'. That certainly gave the exhibitors something to think about! It is fairly typical of the kind of title one may expect from the schedule of a major, national or international competition. Two exhibitors were allowed to stage this for their club.

ARRANGERS
Pat Hutchinson and Mavis Hammond of the Flower Designers' Guild, North of England

The schedule specified that the exhibition was 'to be staged on a base raised 30 cm (12 in) from the floor. Space allowed: width 152 cm (60 in), depth 122 cm (48 in), height 214 cm (84 in). Base and background painted mulberry.'

Inspiration for Interpretation

The arrangers stressed that they spent more time analysing the precise wording of the title, brainstorming and researching than they devoted to any other aspect of the exhibit. They decided that 'evolving' implied change or development that was gradual and that they therefore needed to portray at least three historical designs that demonstrated a gradual change.

The period arrangements needed to be as authentic as possible. In their research they even visited Holland to see an exhibition of Dutch/Flemish flowerpieces. They took their inspiration from an early 17th century Van der Ast painting 'Flowers in a Porcelain Vase' (the small design seen through the wreath); from Jacob van Walscapelle's late 17th century 'Garland of Fruit and Flowers' (for the wreath itself); an early 18th century Sèvres porcelain table-top at London's Victoria and Albert Museum (for the early 18th century French design at the foot of the pedestal); and the rococo paintings by Spaendonck and Boucher in the Wallace Collection (for the exuberant arrangement on the column).

Mechanics

The column, bases and bench were home-made and covered with marble-effect self-adhesive plastic.

The column was a 92 cm (36 in) carpet roll tube with a 23 cm (9 in) cake board top, which fitted down into the tube with three angle brackets. The base of the column was similar, but made of three graded circles of wood.

The low bench, 92 cm (36 in) long by 30 cm (12 in) wide, was raised up 18 cm (7 in) on blocks with 'plaster' feet attached.

The wreath was constructed on an oval wooden frame, painted gold and fixed with angle brackets to its own base of plywood, 50 cm (20 in) by 30 cm (12 in), again covered with marble-effect self-adhesive plastic.

To finish, the column and low arrangement on the right both stood on another 'marble' base.

Plant Material

The delicate little dried arrangement in the glass decanter was chosen to suggest the concept of dying, ageing and fading away. The seedheads were air-dried, the leaves skeletonized and the lily-of-the-valley and white rose were desiccant-dried.

The wreath, which had to suggest maturity and fruitfulness, had quite complicated mechanics. Six small blocks of dry foam were taped at intervals to the front *and* back of the frame. At the base, front and back, between the two supporting angle brackets, were plastic dishes with soaked green foam to hold fresh foliage. The wreath included the following plant material:
Desiccant-dried: roses, dark peonies, striped tulips, narcissi, lily-of-the-valley, muscari
Air-dried: hydrangea (for snowball tree), larkspur, pomegranates, artichoke
Glycerined: oak, acorns
Fresh: peony foliage, melons, black and green grapes, lemons, cherries, sweet potato, apricots, gourds.

The arrangements on the right were to suggest freshness and a new beginning, and the dark mulberry background meant that colours had to be carefully chosen not only to show up well, but also to be in period.

Trails of honeysuckle, peonies (some dark to link with the wreath), catmint, wild rose, larkspur and clematis (C. montana) were used, and quality flowers: stock, carnation, iris, lily. These were arranged in a low 30 cm (12 in) basket at the base and in a Portugese pottery urn, spray-painted to match the background and highlighted with gold, on top of the column.

Accessories

Various accessories were chosen to link with the 'vanitas' objects of Dutch/Flemish paintings (shells, starfish, bee, snail, birds' nest, etc). In the low arrangement two shells link with the rococo style of 18th century France. A pale-green taffeta drape (with important silk tassel, suggesting richness) linked the four arrangements. It was important, as they were very different.

The final placings were agreed but on arrival at the competition, because of the proximity of the next club's space, it was decided to reverse the whole thing, with the pedestal on the right instead of on the left, and the wreath left instead of right. It was a courageous step at that stage and perhaps contributed to its deserved *First Prize*.

IN A STATELY HOME

The decoration of stately homes for festivals in aid of charity has been a feature of NAFAS activities for the past 30 years or more. Sometimes organized by a local flower club, a NAFAS Area or the National Association itself, it has involved many hundreds of arrangers over the years. The opportunity of arranging flowers in a beautiful setting, among priceless treasures, is a special privilege long remembered. It often inspires arrangers to do better work than they thought possible. While many arrangements are purely decorative, some will be interpretative and help to tell the story of the house and its families.

Such festivals are usually designed by one, two or a team of three designers, who then recruit many more arrangers to carry out their designs. One or two viewing days will be held so that arrangers can see the venue and discuss plans and ideas with the designers.

The size, shape, colour and style of each display will, most probably, have already been determined and even some of the plant material may be specified. Props and accessories may be provided or arrangers may be requested to find them. When arrangers go to view, therefore, much has already been decided, but the mechanics, quantities, plant material and other details have still to be worked out.

At an event like this, arrangers must prepare their own lists of containers, mechanics, plant materials and accessories. Notes made on viewing days should be extensive and detailed, accurate in measurement and precise as to colour. Photographs are a great help if they are permitted, so check whether this is the case.

Note also if a step-ladder will be needed for tall placements. Arrangers are usually required to bring plastic sheeting or cloths to protect carpets, floors or furniture while they are working. Slippers or socks may be needed to protect polished floors, marble or tiles.

1 · The display shown here, arranged by *Margot Camp and Edna North of Bookham Flower Arrangement Group*, covered a floor area of approximately 3×2.5 metres (10×8 feet), marked out by a piece of grey felt. It was one of seven large exhibits in the Long Gallery at Sutton Place, Surrey, all of which interpreted some of the owners or incidents in the history of the house.

2 · This display was to depict the building of the house in 1521. Research revealed that the Manor of Sutton was granted by Henry VIII to Sir Richard Weston, a courtier and statesman of skill and distinction. The house he built at Sutton was one of the most important architecturally, after the building of Hampton Court Palace, as it marked the transition from earlier fortified buildings. Sutton Place was constructed in the Italian Renaissance style in brick and ornamental terracotta.

3 · It was important, then, for the arrangers to feature some aspect of the actual building, and they chose the two hexagonal towers that flank the main doorway.

Their two pillars were made from hardboard on a wooden frame and painted in two tones of beige to match the real towers. They were 1.5 metres (5 feet) and 2.15 metres (7 feet) tall and provided the height needed for good proportions to the display.

4 · To suggest both the inside and the outside of the house, paving stones were laid over part of the base. A genuinely old piece of window, with diamond-shaped panes, was fixed to a wooden base so that it stood firmly on the floor.

5 · The colouring was specified by the designers to be in the warm, glowing colours of the brickwork of the house so, as the festival was held at the end of September, the principal flowers were dahlias, lilies and chrysanthemums in rust, orange, apricot, yellow, cream and beige. Ivy, clustered at the top of the towers, trailed down from them to suggest the age of ivy-covered buildings.

6 · The three arrangements were staged at different levels: one on the floor coming through the window, one in a trough on bricks to raise it a little and the tallest on a genuine Tudor oak stool on a velvet draped box to create the feeling of indoor furnishings.

7 · Rosary beads signified the staunch Catholicism of Sir Richard, red fabric suggested the interior of a grand house and a posy of herbs at the foot of the tallest tower was typical of the sweet-smelling Tudor tussy-mussies which were used in an attempt to ward off the plague and to sweeten the air.

8 · The remaining touches emphasized the practical building aspect. In the centre was a group of bricklayer's tools, and the title was displayed in gold on a blue-grey slate.

Other Options

At a different type of year, say in spring or summer, it might be possible to use arrangements in a simpler, more Tudor style with hedgerow and meadow flowers. But this is never easy with an exhibit of this size because the flowers are not large enough to have sufficient impact. More would probably have to be made of the rural setting of the house, with trees and bushes. Then a more obvious division between indoors and out would be likely, and with it the problem of integrating the two parts. The controlled elegance of the exhibit might be lost. Certainly there are many other ways of interpreting 'the building of the house' but the way that was chosen was effective and colourful.

Chapter ten · Review

*L*arger-scale arrangements usually mean working as one of a team, consisting of two or three as a rule, though for a really big exhibit, like the NAFAS stand at London's Chelsea Flower Show, a team of nine is needed. The work may be in a church, cathedral, large exhibition hall, marquee, stately home, art gallery or museum. Each venue will have its own problems (parking, flights of stairs, valuable carpets to be protected, poor lighting, security rules and so on) but each will also have its pleasures.

Preparation on Site

Except for competitive shows, where all the preparation has to be done at home with no chance to see what the staging circumstances will be like, at most other shows or festivals there is at least one briefing or viewing day well beforehand. At this time arrangers can visit, see their site, discuss plans with the designer or chairman of the event *and make their own notes*. This is so important. You will need to take:
● A clipboard with plenty of paper
● Pens and pencils (one with a rubber in the end is invaluable)
● A steel tape measure
● A camera if photography is permitted at the venue (it isn't always)
● Some means of recording colours (I advocate paint colour cards, which are free and usually adequate)

Make copious notes and if there is a tolerable artist in the group, or even if there isn't, make sketches too. Otherwise, you will not remember all the details you need when you start planning back home.

The All-round Island Site

Probably the most difficult of all sites is the one that will be viewed and/or judged from all angles. It does not mean, however, that there must be *equal* interest all around. There will inevitably be a 'front', perhaps where a title is shown or there is a special focus of interest, but there needs to be some interest at the back and sides as well. It is often sensible to divide a circular area into thirds, with a feature in each segment. With an all-round site, there is usually no problem in creating depth. Height, as we have already seen, is always important, but it need not be central and, indeed, can often create greater interest if placed off-centre, because it provides a larger area for the important part of the exhibit and reduces the need to fill up less important areas. Asymmetry can often be more interesting than symmetry.

The Site with Backing Provided

The division of the site by different arrangements and features often results in a very four-square look. Again keep in mind the value of *thirds*. Try to plan features to be a third of the way along the width, depth and height. Use these thirds consciously and you will find they make pleasing divisions and focal points. Take a good look at window-dressing and note how the good windows use this 'designer's grid', as it is called.

Linking the Various Parts

In a team where more than one arranger has a specific area or arrangement to do, each space must be clearly indicated, as proportional relationships can soon get out of hand. The team leader must keep an eye on this or the whole thing gets too crowded. (Most large-scale designs are too crowded.)

Different parts of a large exhibit do need linking. This can be done by repeating a colour or type of plant material or taking line material, such as vines, ivy, cords, through and around the exhibit. Draping can do this too, but don't overdo it or it can dominate. See how well a drape is managed in the arrangements on pages 157 and 159.

An End... and a Beginning

This brings us to the end of the course, which started with a simple bunch in a vase and has led to complicated large displays.

Newcomers to flower arranging may have been surprised to find so many different shapes, sizes and styles to try. Some will appeal more than others, and some that seem less attractive at first will improve on acquaintance. It is, I think, important to keep as open a mind as possible and to let the seeing eye develop gradually, trying this and that as opportunities crop up.

As with any other hobby or craft, practice is everything. No one will do any craft well unless they keep on doing it. That is why joining a flower club is such a good idea – because there you can be involved in what is going on in the flower-arranging world locally, in a wider area, nationally and internationally.

You have a head start already.

The world of flower arranging can open many new doors and is there for you to explore and enjoy.

PLANTS TO GROW FOR FLOWERS OR BERRIES

The plants included here are all excellent to grow for flower arranging, providing flowers and/or berries and sometimes attractive foliage or seedheads too. They can all be grown without a greenhouse.

Spring

A/B *Annual/Biennial* **B** *Bulb* **P** *Perennial* **S** *Shrub*

A/B	B	P	S	PLANT	COLOUR	COMMENT
			✿	*Amelanchier*	*White*	*Young leaves brown*
			✿	*Azalea*	*White, pink, yellow, orange, red*	*Does not tolerate lime*
			✿	*Berberis*	*Yellow, orange*	*Vicious thorns, but worth it*
		✿		*Bergenia*	*White, pink, cerise*	*The leaves are a must, flowers a bonus*
			✿	*Broom (cytisus)*	*White, pink, yellow, orange, red*	*Graceful*
			✿	*Camellia*	*White, pink, red*	*Leaves will glycerine*
	✿			*Daffodil*	*Yellow, cream*	*All sizes and many shapes*
		✿		*Doronicum*	*Yellow*	*Daisy flowers*
		✿		*Euphorbia*	*Green, yellow*	*Many kinds; singe stems*
			✿	*Forsythia*	*Yellow*	*Cut in tight bud*
	✿			*Grape hyacinth (muscari)*	*Blue*	*A rare true blue*
		✿		*Hellebore*	*White, pink, green, burgundy*	*Not easy to condition when young*
	✿			*Hyacinth*	*White, cream, pink, apricot, blue*	*Stem may need wiring*
		✿		*Iris*	*Not pink or red*	*Seedheads useful too*
B				*Lunaria (honesty)*	*Purple, white*	*Silver 'penny' seedheads*
	✿			*Narcissus*	*White, cream, yellow, orange*	*Wide range, as daffodils*
			✿	*Rhododendron*	*Most colours, not true blue*	*Large flowers*
	✿			*Tulip*	*All except blue*	*Every shape and size*
B				*Wallflower (cheiranthus)*	*Cream, yellow, orange, tan, red, purple*	*Can be short-lived perennial*
			✿	*Willow (salix)*	*Silver 'pussy' catkins*	*Cut in bud*

Summer

A/B *Annual/Biennial* B *Bulb* P *Perennial* S *Shrub*

A/B	B	P	S	PLANT	COLOUR	COMMENT
		✿		Acanthus	Mauve, white	Dries well
		✿		Achillea	Yellow, pink, cerise	Dries well
		✿		Alchemilla	Green	Glycerines
		✿		Alliums (onion family)	Mainly mauve	Dries well
A				Amaranthus	Green, red	For drooping heads to dry
Treat as annual				Antirrhinum	All except blue	Glycerine seedheads
A				Aster (callistephus)	Blue, pink, mauve, purple	Shaggy flower heads
		✿		Astilbe	Cream, pink	Tall feathery heads
		✿		Astrantia	Pink, white	Not showy, but useful
A		✿		Campanula	Blue-mauve, purple	Tall spikes
		✿		Crocosmia	Yellow, orange, red	Branching heads
Lift in winter		✿		Dahlia	All except blue	All shapes and sizes
		✿		Day lily (hemerocallis)	Cream, yellow, orange, rust, red	Buds open as flowers fade
		✿		Delphinium	White, blue, mauve, purple	Tall, bold spikes
			✿	Deutzia	Pinky, white	Graceful sprays
B				Foxglove (digitalis)	White, pinky mauve	Lasts well, seedheads glycerine
A				Gladiolus	All except blue	Strong spikes
A				Helichrysum	Orange, cream, yellow, tan, dark red	'Everlasting' to dry
			✿	Hydrangea	White, pink, blue	Use green, fresh, or dry
		✿		Iris	Blue, yellow, white, apricot, buff, purple	Seedheads too
		✿		Kniphofia (red-hot poker)	Red, orange, yellow, cream	Sturdy spike
		✿		Lily (inc. arum lily)	White, yellow, pink, orange, deep red	Grow some if you can
A				Marigold (calendula)	Orange, yellow	Easy-to-grow
			✿	Mock orange (philadelphus)	Cream, white	Strip all leaves
A				Molucella	Green	Glycerines to pale cream
		✿		Phlox	White, pink, red, mauve	Lasts well, greedy feeder
		✿		Pink (dianthus)	White, pink, red, laced	Old-fashioned favourite
			✿	Rose	All except true blue	Large or small, double flowers last well
A				Stock (matthiola)	White, cream pink, mauve, dark red	Useful chunky filler
A				Sweet pea (lathyrus)	Most colours, no true blue	Cut daily to prolong flowers
			✿	Weigela	Pink, dark red	Graceful shrub
A				Zinnia	Green, cream, yellow, orange, red, pink	Stems inclined to crease

Autumn

A/B *Annual/Biennial* B *Bulb* P *Perennial* S *Shrub*

A/B	B	P	S	PLANT	COLOUR	COMMENT
		✿		Aconitum (monkshood)	Blue	'Backbone' material
		✿		Agapanthus	Blue	Seedheads, too
		✿		Artichoke	Mauve, blue	Beautiful grey leaves
		✿		Chrysanthemum	White, cream, yellow, tan, pink, deep red, mauve	Large, small, single and spray
			✿	Cotoneaster, various	Orange, red	Long-lasting berries
				Dahlias	All colours except blue	Many sizes and shapes
		✿		Globe Thistle (echinops)	Blue	Will dry
		✿		Golden Rod (solidago)	Yellow, lemon	Feathery flower heads
		✿		Helenium	Yellow, orange, tan	Daisy flower
		✿		Iris (I. foetidissima)	Orange	Berries in pods
		✿		Michaelmas daisies (aster)	White, pink, mauve, blue	Excellent fillers
			✿	Privet (ligustrum)	Black	Berries a bonus
			✿	Pyracantha	Yellow, orange	Berries
		✿		Sedum	Pink	Long-lasting flower heads
			✿	Snowberry (symphoricarpus)	White, pink	Berries

Winter

A/B *Annual/Biennial* B *Bulb* P *Perennial* S *Shrub*

A/B	B	P	S	PLANT	COLOUR	COMMENT
			✿	Cornus	Red, tan, yellow	Grow for the coloured stems
			✿	Crab apples (malus)	Red, yellow	Long-lasting round fruits
			✿	Daphne	White, pink, mauve	One of the earliest flowers
			✿	Garrya	Grey	Long catkins all winter
			✿	Hazel (corylus)	Yellow catkins	Cut catkins before Christmas
			✿	Holly (ilex)	Red, yellow	A plant for berries and leaves
			✿	Ivy (hedera)	Black	Berries after November
			✿	Jasmine	Yellow	Winter sunshine!
			✿	Laurustinus (viburnum)	Pinky-white	Flowers throughout winter
			✿	Wintersweet (chimonanthus)	Yellow	Sweet-smelling
			✿	Witch hazel (hamamelis)	Yellow	Like clusters of threads

PLANTS TO GROW FOR FOLIAGE

*Here is a flower arranger's list of popular, easy grown small
evergreens and herbaceous plants, that provide attractive
foliage for cutting and interest in the garden.*

Evergreen Foliage

PLANT	COMMENT
Aucuba japonica (Spotted laurel)	Tough leaves splashed with gold. Glycerines to plain black.
Choisya ternata (Mexican orange)	Rosettes of aromatic leaves, white flowers several times a year; variety 'Sundance' has buttercup yellow leaves. Type glycerines to biscuit colour.
Cupressus (Cypress)	Tough feathery foliage. There is a bewildering variety of size, shape, and colour, including blue-grey, lime, yellow, variegated. Beware of choosing one that will grow too large for your garden. Dries and glycerines.
Elaeagnus (Silk bark oak)	E. pungens has sprays of green leaves backed with silver; E. pungens 'Maculata' has gold-splashed leaves all winter.
Eucalyptus gunnii (Cider gum)	Round, grey leaves that glycerine to a rich tan. Tall tree which can be pruned hard or coppiced to keep small.
Garrya elliptica (Tassel bush)	Good evergreen leaves and long grey-green catkins in winter. Both glycerine well.
Hebe (Veronica)	There are a host of hebes of many shapes and sizes, with small leaves useful as fillers and for petite and miniature work.

PLANT	COMMENT
Hedera (Ivy)	A bewildering variety and almost all easy to grow in sun or shade, against a wall or shed, or as ground cover. H. canariensis (white, cream, and grey variegation), H. helix 'Goldheart' (leaves with yellow centres), H. cristata (green frilly-edged leaves, H. colchica 'Sulphur Heart' (also known as 'Paddy's Pride'), which has large green, lime and yellow marked leaves. Ivies will glycerine, but take a long time.
Ilex (Holly)	Hollies are slow-growing and the smoother, less prickly types can be used throughout the year. Favourites include I. x aetaclarensis 'Golden King' and I. aquifolium 'Silver Queen'.
Mahonia (Oregon grape)	M. aquifolium, M. japonica and their hybrids provide useful and sturdy pinnate leaves. They glycerine well to a mid-brown.
Phormium tenax (New Zealand flax)	Tall, leathery, sword-shaped leaves that may be striped and streaked with yellow or pinky-red.
Rosmarinus (Rosemary)	Spires of grey-green narrow leaves with blue flowers in early spring.
Senecio	S. laxifolius and S. greyi are similar and regularly confused. Easily grown from cuttings. The silver buds in early summer are useful as well as the felty leaves.
Skimmia	Slow-growing. Green leathery leaves and red holly-like berries in late summer.

Herbaceous Foliage

PLANT	COMMENT	PLANT	COMMENT
Bergenia	B. cordifolia *is a better-shaped leaf than* B. crassifolia, *and hybrids of* B. stracheyi *colour well in autumn.*	Hosta	*There are now many different hybrids with yellow, lime, blue-green or mid-green leaves, often with white or cream variegation. See them in leaf to choose your favourites. They prefer some shade and need constant protection against snails and slugs.*
Cynara scolymus (Artichoke)	*The large grey leaves are most decorative for large arrangements, as are the blue thistle-like flowers.*		
Heuchera (Coral flower)	*Modern hybrids have round or heart-shaped leaves, which may be dark green, brown or purple.*	Onopordum acanthium (Scotch thistle)	*A biennial plant reaching 180 cm (6 ft) in height, with large silver leaves that are spiny. The thistle-like flowers are similar to those of the artichoke but smaller.*
Helleborus (Hellebore)	*Although grown primarily for their flowers, the leaves of* H. corsicus, H. foetidus *and* H. orientalis *are most useful in arrangements.*		

SUPPLIERS

*Local florist shops, garden centres, nursery men and
town markets will have certain things a flower
arranger needs. Almost all flower clubs have sales tables
where you can buy such items as containers,
mechanics, Christmas items and ribbons, and all clubs will
order* The Flower Arranger, *the NAFAS quarterly
magazine, for you. Flower arrangement shows will have
sales tables for all kinds of flower arranging equipment.
Other suppliers include:*

Containers

CLIVE BROOKER
10 York Avenue, Stanmore, Middx HA7 2HS
Tel: 081-907 5701
Hand-crafted modern ceramic containers

MOIRA CLINCH
10 The Green, Mountsorrel, Leics LE12 7AF
Tel: 0533-375046
Pottery

Mail Order (General)

THE DIDDYBOX
132/134 Belmont Road, Astley Bridge, Bolton
BL1 7AN
Tel: 0204-592405

THE FLOWER CELLAR
161 Wilton Road, Salisbury, Wilts SP2 7JQ
Tel: 0722-321691/333433

FOCAL FLOWERS
Dept F, 17 Cross Flats Avenue, Leeds LS11 7BE
Tel: 0532-774001

Flowers by Rail

K B M SHIRLEY & CO LTD
288 Flower Market, New Covent Garden, London
SW8 5NH
Tel: 071-720 7396

JOHN AUSTIN & CO LTD
305 Flower Market, New Covent Garden, London
SW8 5NB
Tel: 071-720 6835 (4am–1pm)
       071-226 1288 (6pm–9pm)

C H GARDINER
303 Flower Market, New Covent Garden, London
SW8 5NB
Tel: 071-720 7855 (4am–1pm)
Country orders:
Tel: 081-699 5336 or 0732-823583 (7pm–9pm)

Mechanics for Garlands

SIMPLY GARLANDS
51 Albion Road, Pitstone, Beds LU7 9AY
Tel: 0296 661425

Drying and Preserving

FLORA INTERNATIONAL

Products Dept, 77 Bulbridge Road, Wilton,
Salisbury, Wilts SP2 0LE
Tel: 0722-743207
Maureen Foster's Flower-preserving Crystals

IMPRESS

Slough Farm, Westhall, Halesworth, Suffolk
IP19 8RN
Blank cards, etc for pressed flower work

Books

'THE FLOWER ARRANGER' BOOK SERVICE

The Book Secretary, 47 Tenterleas, St Ives,
Huntingdon, Cambs PE17 4QP

FLORA INTERNATIONAL

Products Dept, 77 Bulbridge Road, Wilton,
Salisbury, Wilts SP2 0LE
Tel: 0722-743207
Flora books

Pedestals, Stands

JON EVERSFIELD METAL PRODUCTS

62 Paterson Place, Shepshed, Leics LE12 9RY
Tel: 0509-503698
Wrought iron

COUNTRY CRAFTSMAN IRONWORK LTD

Unit 13, Sidings Industrial Estate, Netley Abbey,
Southampton, Hants SO3 5QA
Tel: 0703-453326/454564
Various stands

READING LIST

*The books selected will give readers a wealth of sound
information and good reading. Some of the earlier ones
are out of print but are usually obtainable from public, or
flower club, libraries.*

General Plant References

Brickell, Chris (ed). *RHS Gardener's Encyclopaedia of
Plants and Flowers*, Dorling Kindersley, 1989

Hay, Roy (ed). *Reader's Digest Encyclopaedia of
Garden Plants and Flowers*, Reader's Digest
Association, 1971 and updates

Philip, Chris. *The Plant Finder*, Hardy Plant Society
(published annually)

General Flower Arranging

Blacklock, Judith. *Teach Yourself Flower Arranging*,
Hodder & Stoughton, 1992

Brack, Edith. *W I Creative Guide to Arranging
Flowers*, WI Books/Unwin Hyman, 1988

Bridges, Derek. *Flower Arranger's Bible*, Century, 1985

Monckton, Shirley. *Arranging Flowers*, Merehurst,
1989

Newnes, Mary. *NAFAS Book of Flower Arranging*,
Ebury Press, 1986

Smith, George. *Flower Decoration*, Webb & Bower,
1988

Taylor, Jean. *Creative Flower Arrangement*, Stanley
Paul, 1973

Taylor, Jean. *Practical Flower Arranging*, Hamlyn,
1973

Vagg, Daphne. *The Flower Arranger's A-Z*, Batsford,
1989

Vagg, Daphne. *Flower Arranging*, Kingfisher, 1980

Webb, Iris. *The Complete Guide to Flower and Foliage
Arrangement*, Webb & Bower, 1979

Drying and Preserving

Black, Penny. *The Complete Book of Pressed Flowers*,
Dorling Kindersley, 1988

Foster, Maureen. *The Art of Preserved Flower
Arrangement*, Collins, 1984

Foster, Maureen. *The Flower Arranger's Encyclopaedia
of Preserving and Drying*, Blandford, 1988

Gordon and Lorimer. *The Complete Guide to Drying
and Preserving*, Webb & Bower, 1982

Newnes, Mary. *NAFAS Arranging Everlasting
Flowers*, Ebury Press, 1987

Scott and Beazley. *Making Pressed Flower Pictures*,
Batsford, 1979

Scott and Beazley. *Pressed Flowers through the
Seasons*, Batsford, 1983

Freestyle and Abstract

Aaronson, Marian. *Design with Plant Material*,
Grower Books, 1972

Aaronson, Marian. *Flowers in the Modern Manner*,
Grower Books, 1982

Brack, Edith. *Flower Arrangement – Freestyle*,
Whitethorn Press, 1977

Brack, Edith. *Modern Flower Arranging*, Batsford,
1982

Burger, Paola and Loli Marsano. *Scultura Floreale*,
Idea Books Edizione, Milan (Italian text with
separate English translation)

Church Flowers

Keith, Margaret (ed). *Flower Festivals*, NAFAS, 1992

Macqueen, Sheila. *Church Flower Arranging*, Hyperion/Ward Lock, 1982

Taylor, Jean. *Church Flowers, Month by Month*, Mowbray, 1979

Taylor, Jean. *Flowers in Church*, Mowbray, 1976

Wedding Flowers

Mann, Pauline. *Wedding Flowers*, Batsford, 1985

McNicol, Pamela. *Flowers for Weddings*, Batsford, 1990

Show Work

NAFAS BOOKLETS
NAFAS Handbook of Schedule Definitions
NAFAS Judges' Manual
NAFAS Show Guide

Napper, Mary. *Flower Arranging for Shows*, Batsford, 1984

History

Berrall, Julia S. *A History of Flower Arrangement*, Thames & Hudson, 1969

Cooke, Dorothy and McNicol, Pamela (eds). *A History of Flower Arranging*, Heinemann, 1989

Newdick, Jane. *Period Flowers*, Charles Letts, 1991

Vagg, Daphne. (ed). *Guide to Period Flower Arranging*, NAFAS, 1992

Floristry

Coleman, Rona. *The Floristry Handbook*, Batsford

Coleman, Rona. *The Seasonal Florist and Flower Arranger*, Christopher Helm, 1990

Magazines

Flora, Maureen Foster, Wilton, Salisbury, Wiltshire (published six times a year)

The Flower Arranger, NAFAS (published quarterly). Obtainable from flower clubs or by subscription from the printers, Taylor Bloxham, Nugent Street, Leicester

NAFAS Leaflets

The National Association publishes 20 inexpensive leaflets on all the basic aspects of flower arranging, including one on colour theory specially compiled for the flower arranger. Contact the Publications Distribution Officer, NAFAS, 21 Denbigh Street, London SW1V 2HF.

ACKNOWLEDGEMENTS

*A book for a large association like NAFAS involves many
people besides the arrangers themselves. Their names
appear on the pages describing their work. Some
50 arrangers were involved, none of whom had
arrangements in the two previous NAFAS books
published by Ebury Press.*

Special thanks are due to the hosts and hostesses who welcomed us and made photography days a pleasure in spite of the upheaval we created:

The Vicar and Churchwarden of Holy Cross
Church, Uckfield, Sussex
Elizabeth and Ian Hunter-Craig
Betty and Den James
Gwen and Geoff Mason
Shirley and Dennis Monckton
Somerset Country Furniture, Ilchester
Annette and John Stoker
The Headmaster and the Rector of Stonyhurst
College
Dallas and Alan Taylor
Molly and Colin Watson

Others who helped to set up these days were the Chairmen of three Areas of NAFAS: Avril Hill of Kent, Dorothy Kay of Sussex and Josephine Yates of the North-West; Janet Hayton, Chairman of the NAFAS Education Committee; Arthur and Joy Sutton who helped with staging; and Brenda Smith who was a splendid helper on one of the days. Ray Cole, Chairman of the NAFAS Photography Committee, organized some show photographs at the 1992 national competitions, and Jill Grayston, editor of *The Flower Arranger*, generously lent two transparencies.

Marie-Louse Avery, our photographer, was also our hostess on two occasions. To her, and to her helper, Gloria Nicol, my grateful thanks for their care, patience and good company. Additional photography is by Howard Nutt (page 159), Roy Smith (page 161) and John Vagg (page 135).

The first all-colour flower arrangement book I ever possessed (and still enjoy) was the *Ilford Colour Book of Flower Decoration* by Joan Groves of the Constance Spry Flower School. It was published in 1964 by Ebury Press. It is a tribute to the publishers' loyalty to the subject that they are still publishing flower arrangement books with fine colour photography. To them, to Denise Bates, their editorial director, and to Alison Wormleighton, their editor, NAFAS says 'thank you'.

Daphne Vagg
for NAFAS, The National Association of Flower Arrangement Societies of Great Britain
21 Denbigh Street, London SW1V 2HF, England.

INDEX

Page references in *italic* refer to illustrations